THE LAST TIBETAN KINGDOM

ROSE LANE

THE LAST TIBETAN KINGDOM

A JOURNEY IN SEARCH OF HOME

HEMBURY
—BOOKS—

Copyright © Rose Lane 2025
First published by Hembury Books in 2025
hemburybooks.com.au
info@hemburybooks.com
Paperback ISBN 9781923517172
Ebook ISBN 9781923517165

The moral right of the author has been asserted.
All rights reserved. No portion of this book may be reproduced in any form without permission from the author and publisher, except as permitted by Australian copyright law.

 A catalogue record for this book is available from the National Library of Australia

For Neville

All things are subject to interpretation;
whichever interpretation prevails at a given time
is a function of power and not truth.

FRIEDRICH NIETZSCHE

Contents

Prologue 11
Chapter 1: **Home** 13
Chapter 2: **Preparation** 23
Chapter 3: **After the Earthquake** 32
Chapter 4: **To Pokhara** 42
Chapter 5: **Jomsom** 48
Chapter 6: **Kagbeni** 54
Chapter 7: **Into Restricted Territory** 61
Chapter 8: **Tsele** 69
Chapter 9: **Samar** 72
Chapter 10: **Lha Gyal Lo** 78
Chapter 11: **Apple Pie at the Royal Hotel** 86
Chapter 12: **Tragmar** 91
Chapter 13: **Lo Gekar** 98
Chapter 14: **The Walled City** 103
Chapter 15: **The Buddha Who is to Come** 115

Chapter 16: **To See Tibet** 133

Chapter 17: **Out of Sight** 139

Chapter 18: **One Last Night With the Russians** 143

Chapter 19: **To Dhe** 147

Chapter 20: **Yara** 153

Chapter 21: **A Flying Monk and a Dangerous Goddess** 158

Chapter 22: **Tsarang** 168

Chapter 23: **Life and Death** 177

Chapter 24: **Shyanmochen** 180

Chapter 25: **Chhuksang** 186

Chapter 26: **The Final Leg** 190

Chapter 27: **Pokhara Again** 193

Chapter 28: **Escaping Kathmandu** 195

Author's Notes 203

Bibliography 204

Acknowledgments 207

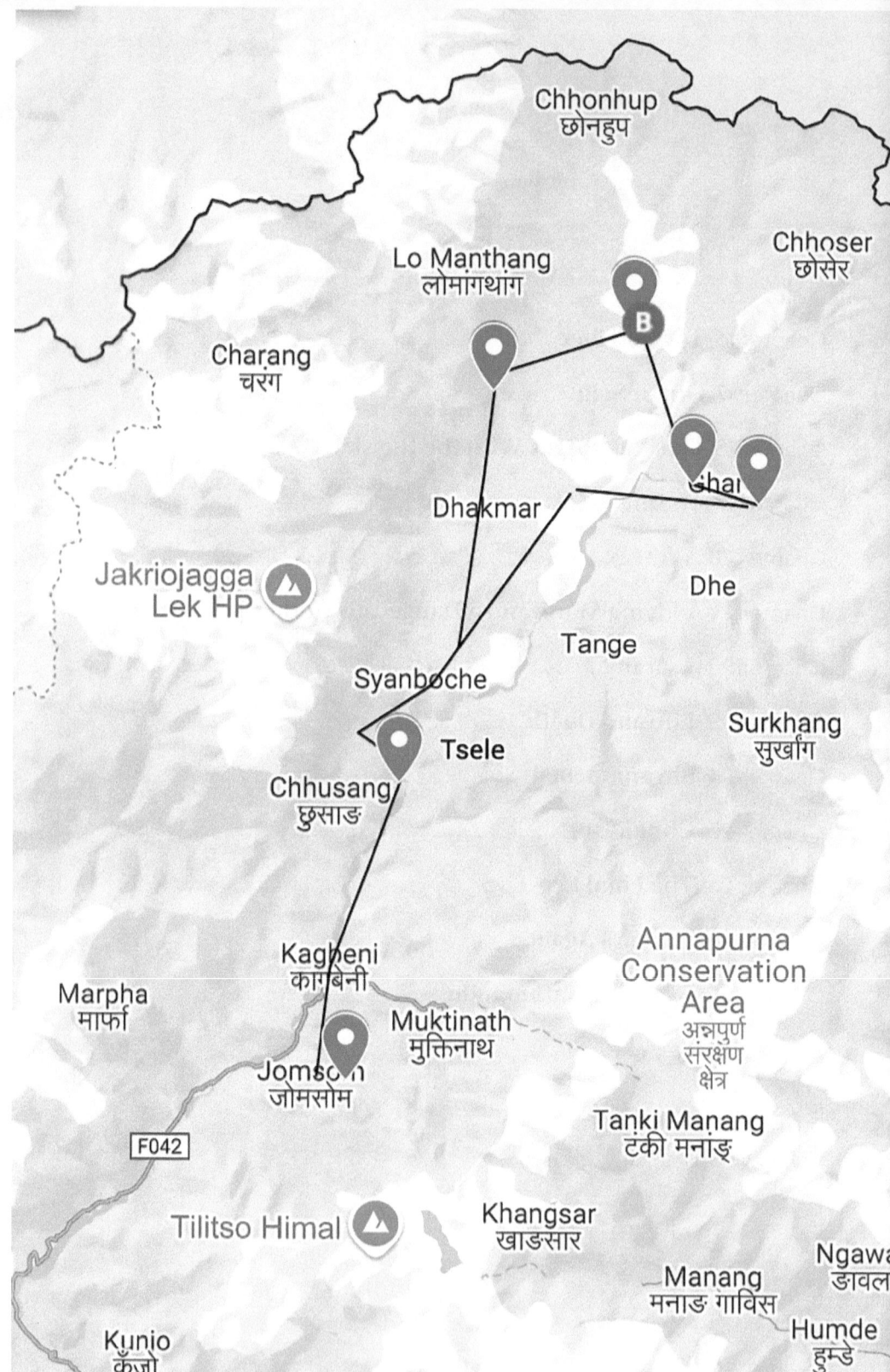

Prologue

Just before midnight I was awoken by ferocious growling and barking. It was right outside the door where the dog belonging to the owners of the lodge was chained up, a great Tibetan mastiff with matted fur and a big, heavy face. It sounded as though if I opened the door it would tear me to pieces. Other dogs around the village were also barking. I sat up in bed, pulled aside the thin curtain and looked out on the hill that rose above us under the light of an almost full moon. It was like daylight outside and the stunted bushes stood out clearly on the hillside. I sat and watched. Earlier that day, on our way from Lo Manthang I had noticed large cat paw prints heading in the opposite direction to us.

"Snow Leopard?" I'd asked our assistant guide, Dipak.

"Ya," he'd replied. "Big one."

So I sat and looked out at that barren landscape and listened to the frightening growls of the dog outside my door, hoping to see a leopard, but for the first time in my life I felt truly grateful for the safety of shelter: thick walls that protected me from whatever predator lurked outside. Unless the danger dwelt within; I was a long way from home now, but that was kind of the point.

CHAPTER 1

Home

I was three years old when I decided to leave home. I was outside playing in the back yard while my mother hung the washing on the clothesline when I made the decision. It didn't occur to me to make any preparations, nor to let anyone know; I just went. When she realised I was missing, my mother mounted a search party comprising my sisters and some neighbours. I was found a couple of blocks away.

"Where do you think you're going," one of my sisters asked.

"I'm going off to see the world," was my reply.

As I got I was older, I kept leaving home. I was constantly at the neighbours' houses. One rainy night, I put on my yellow raincoat and hat and headed next door. What can the neighbour have thought when they saw me standing on their doorstep in the pouring rain at nine o'clock at night? On weekends I helped rake leaves with the widow on one side, and on weekdays I helped hang out the washing with the lady on the other side. She had a toy clothesline, a miniature Hill's Hoist, and she would put the wet handkerchiefs in an ice cream tub and I would peg these on my little clothesline while she hung out the big clothes. When I finished I would hide and she would pretend she couldn't find me.

So where was my mother while these women were effectively minding me? What was going on in my own home that I felt the need at such a young age to get the hell out of there?

I am the youngest of six children. No, actually I am the youngest of eight children. My brother was the first born, two years later a sister, two years later another sister, two years later Rose. The other Rose, the one of whom there are no photos, no nothing, no sign she ever existed except for a tiny, pale, blue-tiled grave. I don't know whether Mum even saw her third daughter. It was the fifties. I imagine Mum was sedated, and when she woke, told to forget about this child she had carried for nine months, had felt moving restless growing limbs inside her, that had kept her awake, sat on her bladder, crept into her dreams, the imagined fourth child, the imagined family of six. No doubt she was told to go home and have a new one.

So a year later another girl was born. Two years later another. Then two years later finally another boy, David. Mum and Dad never told my siblings the other Rose ever existed, not until they were forced to when David also died suddenly, setting off a cascade of grief and recrimination that has echoed down through the years and still continues today.

So you see, I was born into a mess of grief, to a mother who kept on the move, cleaning, cooking, washing, ironing, sewing, answering the phone for Dad's veterinary practice, shopping, and, at the end of the day when forced to stop, drank whisky—only one or two—enough to hold off that dark thing always lurking in the shadows, waiting to drag her down. And to her credit, my mother never did give into that demon. She carried on, a dutiful wife and mother. Stalwart and determined, my mother built a fortification around her to ensure nothing else could get her.

※ ※ ※

When I was still at school, my father subscribed to a set of encyclopaedias, one a month until you had the whole set. They were called *The World and Its People* and they were colourful and glossy. I used to sit on the cool linoleum floor in his office and pull them one by one off the shelf and read about places far away from Bellingen, the small country town where I was born and raised. I remember reading about a place called Iceland, which I'd heard of and assumed was like a small version of Antarctica, icy and uninhabited. But it wasn't. People lived there. There were towns. Why did we never hear about this place? I determined to go there. It became an obsession.

"Why would you want to go to Iceland?" people would say. "Isn't it just ice?"

In 1993, my husband Neville and I made the obligatory Australian pilgrimage to London to work. After a stint at nannying, I went back to nursing. I signed up with an agency and got some home nursing jobs, one of which was looking after a demented old woman who used to go crazy and hurl abuse at me and pull my hair. I worked three and a half twelve-hour shifts a week with her and another six hours with a more pleasant lady. For forty-eight hours work I was paid one hundred and sixty pounds; our rent was four hundred pounds a month. I left home at seven in the morning and got home at nine at night. Fortunately, Neville was earning better money but things were still pretty tight. We rented a one bedroom flat above the high street in Crystal Palace and the for first month, January, we had no heating and no hot water as the boiler was broken and it took the real estate agent that long to fix it. It was all a bit grim.

"But we still have to get to Iceland," I said to Neville as we strolled through the streets of London one grey wintery day.

"We can't afford it," he replied.

"Well, I'm going to Iceland," I said.

To get myself through the long days with the mad woman, I pored over my Lonely Planet Guide, *Iceland, Greenland, and The Faroe Islands* learning Icelandic pronunciation, what foods they ate, and what sights we would see.

Eventually we managed to save up enough money and the trip was booked. I called the nursing agency to give my notice and they demanded to know why I was quitting.

"I'm going to Iceland," I said.

"Iceland?" they scoffed, "Why would you want to go there?"

✲ ✲ ✲

I wonder if that three-year-old me gave any thought to her return after exploring the world and, if she did, whether she expected to just walk back into the yard and find her mother still hanging washing on the line. In 2013 my mother called to say she was putting the house on the market and would be moving in with my eldest sister two hours away. Although I knew in my head this was inevitable, it still hurt. I tried being Buddhist about it (even though I'm not).

"Oh well," I said. "Nothing is meant to last forever."

"Well yes," my mother replied, "but it's not much comfort."

It was no comfort at all and the loss of the only home I'd known as a child left me finding it difficult to get out of bed and to eventually sitting in a therapist's room meekly accepting the tissues she offered, trying not to sob uncontrollably. The loss of my "home" even though I hadn't lived there for years and now had a home and family of my own, was incomprehensible, as though I'd woken to find the sky had gone or the ground underneath me. If all turned to shit where was I to go if I couldn't go home? Where was my safe place?

One of the tenets of Buddhist philosophy is the notion of impermanence. It is futile to cling to the things of this world because nothing lasts forever. To demonstrate this, Tibetan monks spend days making intricate sand mandalas. Using metal, hollow cone-shaped implements with ridges along the tops, they painstakingly shake coloured sand, almost grain by grain onto a surface marked by a template. So doing they create the most beautiful intricate designs. The detail is breath-taking and the colours sublime. It's a fascinating thing to watch in progress and the result is mesmerising. It takes several days to make a sand mandala, but almost as soon as it is completed it is swept away.

It made no sense at all that I should be so distraught at losing a home I hadn't lived in for almost thirty years and in which I had never been happy. Never. My therapist asked me what happy memories I had growing up there, her pen poised to record my answers. I couldn't come up with any. I tell myself I'm being melodramatic when I say this, but I seriously can't find any truly happy memories, probably because I always felt like an outsider.

In *Brother and Sisters: coping with grief and loss* Zoë Krupka writes about the death of her younger brother and how it has affected her throughout her life. She writes about how the death of a child can affect their siblings, including those born after the event, and for the first time I read words that express the way I have always felt within my family:

> Without an acknowledgement of their connection to the sibling who died before them, they can become invisible in the family, almost an outsider, and something of a mystery to themselves.

It was never acknowledged that David was my brother too. I never knew him, I had no memories of him, I didn't experience those awful days after he died, so I had no share in that enormous, all-encompassing thing that bound my siblings and my parents. I had never known the before, so had no clear understanding of the after. I grew in the same womb, slept in the same cot in the same room, sat in the same high chair, probably looked a bit like him, but the unspoken thing that inhabited the very air of that house was "you have no right to share in our grief. You have no right to call him your brother. You are and forever will be a thing apart from us". It was as though I had shown up to a party ready to join in the fun, not realising something terrible had happened. I was the excited one who arrives raring to go, but whom everyone stares at and turns away.

I once remarked to my mother that she must have been annoyed to find herself pregnant again at forty-four. "No," she replied. "I was quite pleased actually."

My siblings doted on me and there are as many photos of me as my brother, the first-born. In fact, my brother made up a photo album of everyone's baby photos. There are pages of him, a few of my eldest sister, and so on decreasing until the fourth sister only gets a page and a half. Then I fill the rest of the book and the leftovers of me are stuffed loose inside the back cover. There are none of David. But the doting wained as I grew up and was no longer cute. I was gradually excluded, probably not consciously, but merely because I was so much younger. I was sent to do some chore if there was anything serious to be discussed. Unfortunately, as I grew older they all forgot I was no longer the baby. There are still some things I've only gleaned from fragments and whispers but, maybe because I forget I'm not still a baby, I'm not game to ask about.

As I write this, I feel like I am peeling off my skin, layer by layer, shedding the barrier that has set me apart from my siblings, breaking down the wall they built between us, and in doing so, I am exposing myself to their wrath, leaving a layer that is pink and new and easily hurt. How dare I knock at their walled-off sanctum of grief and fading memory. Even worse, how dare I write about unspoken things, forbidden things I couldn't possibly understand. Things that were never spoken in order to protect Mum. No one was ever allowed to upset Mum. I never heard her screams that night or watched her walk around the house like a ghost afterwards. I was not there. I don't belong.

I have never expressed how I felt about my other brother, never felt I had any right to. Over the years I have many times wished he were still alive, even missed him. What would my life have been like if I had had a sibling close in age? We would have been at primary school together. Perhaps he would have been my protector. Instead of being an appendage, separated from the rest of my siblings by a gap of eight years, I would simply have been the last of a continuous line. Maybe we would have listened to the same music. We would have had the same cultural references, watched the same TV programs. I did share some of these things with my sister closest in age, but the others felt like auxiliary parents. In fact, that's kind of what they were. I have not a single memory of my mother bathing me, playing with me, or reading me a story. My sisters did all of those things as far as I can remember, which was not unusual in large families. My brother, seventeen years older than me, was away at boarding school and then university while I was growing up. I have no memory of him actually living with us, making him more of an uncle than a brother.

When they all played Monopoly or Squatter, I was too young to join in. By the time I was old enough to play those games there was no one left at home to play with. I became a cross between a youngest child and an only child.

So what was it that I was sad about losing when faced with the loss of that home? My therapist hypothesised that in the absence of any*one* to attach to I had attached myself to the building itself. For better or worse, that house was home, meaning it was the one constant in my life, the place I could always return to and find nothing changed, however miserable. Like a form of Stockholm Syndrome, it was the source of my unhappiness, but it was also my refuge.

At twelve, like most of my siblings, I was sent away to boarding school. This was a normal transition in my family. Both my parents went to boarding school, my father at the age of ten. I cried for most of the first year, but by my fourth year, I was crying the night before I had to go home. After nearly four years away, I had no friends in my home town and my parents had little interest in me and, being so old (they were both mid-forties when I was born), little connection to my world. Boarders went home every fourth weekend and for holidays; I came to dread it. On one occasion I returned home to find my mother had completely emptied my room of all the things that had made it mine: pictures, knick-knacks, toys. She'd had a clean out. "I thought I'd get rid of all the rubbish, especially the things that hold dust and make your asthma and hay-fever worse." Sentimentality was a luxury that she had long ago ceased to indulge in.

And yet, that home, that never felt like home, was still, in my mind, my safe place. After reading *The Lord of the Rings* I even started to think of it as Rivendell, the elves haven, safe from the outside world. And the town of Bellingen even now, retains a mythical quality for me. It sits in a lush, green valley in northern New South Wales, cut through by the Bellinger River. Its peaceful beauty attracted the hippies in the seventies, much to my parents chagrin, and many artists have settled there over the years. It's a haven of natural therapies and organic everything. As I was growing up, alongside the basic shops—the butcher, the clothes shops, the small department stores, the pharmacy—signs appeared advertising things like chakra balancing and aura reading. One of my sisters, who did almost all of high school at the local school, had some hippieish friends. I remember driving out to Kalang with her, an area west of Bellingen where the road runs out into the bush. We visited some people living in a shack, sleeping on an unmade mattress on the floor, which was bare boards splattered with paint. They didn't have enough glasses so we drank out of jars. I was quietly horrified and a bit nervous. I couldn't trust people who lived in houses with unmade beds and inadequate crockery. Even seeing clean dishes stacked on a dish rack that hadn't been dried and put away made me suspicious. At home, everything was always in order: clean, tidy, and organised. Always.

That feeling of safety may also have something to do with the fact that I was a sickly child and my mother always cared for me diligently when sick. I was asthmatic and she was up to me many winter nights when I woke coughing and wheezing. Whenever I was sick, she was immediately onto it. And she was on the constant lookout for a cure. When yoga came to Bellingen in the seventies, and she read that it helped people with asthma, she signed me up. She took me to specialists, I had my tonsils removed, we tried different medications, but nothing helped.

In Traditional Chinese Medicine, the lungs are associated with grief. Given that I have been asthmatic since early childhood, I've often wondered whether it was my mother's grief, which would still have been at its most raw and painful while she was pregnant with me, that caused the weakness in my lungs. No one else in my family has ever suffered from asthma.

My mother was also an excellent cook, and never slacked off when it came to getting dinner on the table. So you could always rely on a good meal, every night of the week, right on six-thirty. So if my poor health was always attended to, there was always good food prepared, and there was a place for everything and everything in its place, perhaps this is why I felt safe.

At the age of nineteen, I descended into a deep depression. At the time I'd never heard of depression, so I actually didn't know what was wrong with me. I was in my second year at university, had moved into a share house with friends I made at our residential college in first year, but we didn't really hang out, and I found myself quite alone in the world. I was studying an arts degree because I didn't know what else to do, so I was in too many different and changing classes to spend enough time with the same people to make friends. My physical response to my misery was to completely lose my appetite. I had anorexia in the purest sense of the word, not anorexia nervosa: I didn't think I was fat, and wasn't trying to lose weight. I simply couldn't eat. I would force myself to eat some toast in the morning, but it would often come straight back up. I had no one to turn to and knew my family would be no help, but I called home anyway because what else could I do? By that time I weighed thirty-eight kilograms, my period had stopped, and I became dizzy if I stood up for too long.

"Well I suppose you'd better come home," my mother said, after questioning me about what the problem was and I really couldn't answer. I didn't know.

I sat at the kitchen table while she moved about the kitchen, questioning me as she went. What was wrong? Was it my studies? Was I worried about them? Was I finding it all too hard?

"I'm lonely," I finally came out with. "I don't have any friends."

"Well I don't have any friends either," she shot back at me.

She called one of my sisters. "Rose is worried about university," she told her. "Maybe you could have a chat with her," and she handed the phone to me.

※ ※ ※

On the last morning at home, before it was sold, I touched the walls and the doorposts, and tried to do a kind of Marie Kondo expression of gratitude to the house. I said goodbye to my mother and as I drove down the driveway, turned right into our street, left at the corner where my sisters used to cross over and walk across a farm to school, across the small bridge near the house where they shot our dog with a slug gun for walking on their vegetable garden, turned right, and headed out of town for the last time, I began to sob. And as I drove and cried, I set myself a new goal as though to fill the void, so I had somewhere to head towards; whatever it took, I would get to the walled city Lo Manthang in Nepal. Having lost the anchor of home it was as though I needed to fix upon some other unchanging and seemingly permanent thing, otherwise I would sink.

CHAPTER 2

Preparation

In 2010 we decided to take our three sons somewhere completely different so they could see not everyone in the world lived comfortable lives like us. It had to be somewhere difficult but not dangerous. I'd always wanted to see the Himalayas so we settled on Nepal. It was during my research about this country that I read about a walled city on the Tibetan plateau in a remote part of Nepal that had been there for seven hundred years, largely untouched, the inhabitants still living much the same way they had for those seven centuries. How could I have never heard of Lo Manthang? Googling elicited only ads for trekking and there was just a short entry on Wikipedia. I tried to find a book but the only one I could find was written in the 1960s by a French adventurer called Michel Peissel; long out of print, it was going for as much as four hundred dollars on the internet. I tried the local library but they didn't have it, but I kept searching and I did eventually find a more reasonably priced copy online. When it arrived I felt like I was opening a sacred tome.

The map of Nepal looks like a wobbly rectangle turned on its side. About halfway along its northern border there is a bump that pushes up into Tibet. This is Mustang, an area that reaches from the town of Jomsom in the south to the Tibetan border. To get there one must travel through a gap in the Himalayas, between the Dhaulagiri and Annapurna ranges. In eighteen minutes by plane from Pokhara, you travel from lush, humid green to mountainous desert. That bump in the border is a visual representation of the historical incorporation of Mustang into Nepal, as though a lasso were thrown around it. The Kingdom of Lo, as it was known, was formerly part of the area of Ngari in Tibet but annexed by Nepal in the late eighteenth century by the Gorkhas (the royal family for which the Gurkha soldiers were later named) looking to expand their territory.

Foreigners weren't allowed into Nepal until the 1950s, and travel to Upper Mustang, the area north of the village of Kagbeni, was still prohibited until 1992. Visitors had to be chaperoned by guides and government officials, and numbers were restricted. This was partly because of the guerrilla war that had been fought with China by Khampa warriors, Tibetan resistance fighters trying to hold onto Tibet. Mustang was used as a base for its easy accessibility across the border. The fighting ended in the late sixties but it was still a sensitive area. And there was also a desire to keep foreigners out of what was a culturally and historically sensitive area.

In 2015 travelling to Lo Manthang was not like travelling to Iceland. If you had enough money you could just drop onto the plateau in a helicopter—which felt to me like cheating— or you could endure a rough eight-hour jeep ride that may or may not get you there, depending on weather conditions and the time of year. Otherwise you had to walk. At the time of writing you still have to pay an entry fee of five hundred U.S. dollars per person, which will buy you ten days. If you want to stay longer it costs fifty dollars a day, but the time is limited, and you must employ a registered guide. Unlike my husband, Neville, who can walk for days on end without tiring, anything more than half an hour and I'm turning around. I class myself as feeble. I was a sickly child, and though not a sickly adult, I lack stamina. I've tried to overcome this by signing up for gyms or undertaking self-imposed exercise programs at home, and at first they go well, but three weeks is my limit. I crash with exhaustion and am all but bed-ridden for a week. I get up and try again, but at the three-week mark it happens again.

So how was I to manage a journey of twelve days, at altitude, in a mountainous landscape requiring passage over high passes? Why on horseback of course.

"And being a country girl you would have done a lot of horse-riding," said a friend when I announced this at a gathering.

I shook my head.

"What?! But you've ridden a horse before?"

"I've been *on* a horse, just for a go, but I've never actually been horse-riding."

At this they all fell about laughing.

So I decided to have some lessons.

I don't think many middle-aged women have beginner horse-riding lessons and I got the impression from my young instructor that I was a bit of a hopeless case but she'd persevere. I signed up for six fortnightly lessons. All I knew about horses was that you shouldn't walk up close behind them or they'll kick you. Jasper, the school horse, was a long-suffering creature and I often felt sorry for him having to put up with me speeding him up and slowing him down, steering him around obstacles, digging my heels into his side, rising to the trot at the wrong time. The instructor, with studied patience, would constantly remind me,

"Legs on!..Hands down. Try letting go of the saddle...Elbows in... Heels down...Core muscles on and up, down, up down...ok lets just stop for a minute."

She never seemed pleased to see me, but by about the fourth lesson, when I looked like I was finally getting the hang of it, she started to seem like she didn't dread my lesson any more. I got that I needed to grip on with my legs, not just hang onto the reins for grim death, that I needed to hold myself upright in the saddle, shoulders back and looking where I was going instead of at Jasper's head.

"I won't be there with you on the trek. If you don't look where you're going you'll hit a tree branch, or go off the edge of a cliff. And do you have a helmet?"

I did not have a helmet and was not going to buy one for a twelve day trek.

"It's just not worth it to not wear one," she said.

So I borrowed one and took it to my final class.

"This is no good," she said examining the inside and reading the Australian Standards label. "It was made in 2006. It's out of date so it's not safe. I replace mine every two years."

I'd been wearing one of the school helmets. I'd even brought a bicycle helmet along to one lesson thinking this would do.

"That's a bicycle helmet," she said.

"Yes."

"It's no good. I can't let you wear it for your lesson. It's just not strong enough. If a horse stomped on your head it'd crush this helmet."

I tried to imagine how I could end up in a situation where the horse would actually be stomping on my head, particularly on the trek when I would be just going along at walking pace, since Neville and our guide would be walking. I couldn't imagine myself galloping off alone into the wilds of Upper Mustang, being thrown off and the horse running up and stomping on my head.

In the end I figured I could risk the out of date helmet.

"Well put some of the padding from your bicycle helmet inside it to add a bit of cushioning."

I didn't bother.

In planning our trip to Lo Manthang I pored over the map, looking at the various routes we could take. One way I could tell if it was much travelled was by looking on Google Earth to see how many photos had been uploaded from a particular area. None was a good sign. There were quite a few photos going up the Kali Gandaki gorge, but none out in the barren area to the east. We could trek up the river gorge as is the usual route, but return through the remotest country, far from settlements, travelling through country rarely, if ever, visited.

When I read that the English travel writer, Freya Stark, had, at the age of four, packed a bag and headed off with the same ambition as three-year-old me, I felt an instant connection, a validation even. Perhaps I was of the same fearless ilk. My wanderlust was later inspired by my heroine, the Irish travel writer Dervla Murphy, who at the age of 31, having cared for her sick mother since she was forced to leave school at 14, got on her bicycle in Dublin and rode it to Delhi. She had had this dream since she was 10, having been gifted a bicycle and an atlas for her birthday. If she could ride around her local surrounds, she reasoned, then if she kept doing it she would eventually make it to India. It was 1963 when she set off. The diary she kept became the best-seller *Full Tilt*.

"I've given Pradeep the suggested routes we want to take, but he says returning via the remote one would be difficult because we'd have to carry all our food and water and they're very long days," Neville told me. Pradeep was our guide.

"Ohhh!" I whined, "but I want to go the hardest way." I smiled, knowing Neville knew it was wishful thinking.

"Well, we can go that way if you *really want*," he replied, "Pradeep's just warning us it'll be long and difficult."

The *Lonely Planet* guide similarly cautioned against choosing this route. Neville never told me what I should or shouldn't do and he would take the difficult route if that's what I really wanted; it was my trip, my decision. But I gave in and accepted the more travelled route, knowing I'd probably end up hating it anyway, assuming I even made it. And that's what it felt like, taking the easier option, a cop out. Why couldn't I be like Dervla, like Freya, like Michel Peissel?

During our first trip to Nepal I bought a postcard of Mustang and when I got home I pinned it to the cork board in my office so I would keep thinking about it, and help firm my resolve to go there. At that time it felt like a fantasy. I mean, it was far from anywhere, difficult to get to, expensive, and how was my feeble body going to make it? Still I kept telling myself I was going to get there. There was no other way to see it. There weren't any travel shows on TV about Lo Manthang, no documentaries. I even set up a Google alert to catch anything that came up, but if it did ping, it was usually an ad for trekking.

I have been asked a few times why I wanted to see it. It's hard to answer. Most people say they wouldn't bother going through such an uncomfortable journey to see anything. I feel as though if there's no effort involved it's probably not worth it. Many people are happy with a fully organised guided tour; I can think of nothing worse. But what was it about Lo Manthang? Well the words "walled, mediaeval city," are part of it, that and the fact that this extraordinary place was so little documented. While I knew it wasn't the case, I felt like a bit of an explorer going into unknown territory. It's there for anyone to find on Google Earth, and you will see an L-shaped construction in the middle of a dusty, brown landscape, with nothing for kilometres around. But I'm still not answering the question. I wouldn't climb Mt Everest, but others risk their lives to do it. I like a challenge that's not totally beyond my ability and I think doing so to see something truly unique is worth it. Maybe that's it: Lo Manthang is truly unique. It's the only walled city built in the middle ages that is still lived in in the same way as when it was built, by descendent generations, and even had its own royal family living in a palace until shortly after our visit. There was still a feudal system in place in as much as the people still worked the King's land. Tibetan Buddhism is still part of everyday life just as religion was in the west during the middle ages. Here was a place apart, preserved in time, but it couldn't hide from the world forever, as evidenced by an episode of ABC's Foreign Correspondent that aired a year before our trip, called "The Road". It was about the road being built through Mustang to the Tibet border, making the whole area more accessible. Now I knew I had to get there as soon as possible, before it disappeared forever.

If I was trying to be a real explorer like Dervla and Freya, I would have gone by myself. I would have organised the whole thing myself and left my family behind without another thought. This is what the male explorers did. Michel Peissel left his heavily pregnant wife behind (which may go some way to explain why they eventually divorced). He didn't know when or even if he would return. Peter Matthiessen went off to look for snow leopards not long after his wife died, leaving his young son behind with the promise that he'd be home for Thanksgiving. He wasn't. Paul Theroux admits to being away a lot when his children were growing up. He went off on his *Great Railway Bazaar* odyssey leaving behind an unhappy wife. They too eventually divorced.

The ladies, on the other hand, didn't generally marry and certainly didn't leave behind children. Freya Stark and Alexandra David-Need both married but the marriages didn't last and neither had children. Dervla Murphy never wanted to marry, but she decided she did want a child; once her daughter was old enough, she took her along on her adventures. You'll find an extensive list of female explorers or travellers on Wikipedia but you won't find such a list of male explorers; male explorers are a given. Female travellers, particularly travel writers, tend to get different treatment compared to their male counterparts. Mention female travel writing and *Eat, Pray, Love* is often what springs to people's minds before they make some kind of derisive remark. I have never considered *Eat, Pray, Love* a travel book. Elizabeth Gilbert is not a travel writer. Her book is more about a woman leaving everything behind to discover who she is and what she really wants. It isn't really about the places she visited. Elizabeth Gilbert's book was a runaway success because so many women identified with her feeling of being trapped by marriage and the expectation to have children.

When I read it I totally got it. At that time I was firmly tied to the kitchen sink. When it was published in 2007, my sons were thirteen, eleven, and nine. I was driving an average of a thousand kilometres a week doing the school run and to music lessons and soccer training. We had no family around to help out, no grandparents to drop them to or to help with school pickups. Hence, why I didn't have a day job. I had worked as a nurse until 2004, but found it too difficult juggling everything and besides, looking after very sick children was taking its toll; I was struggling to leave their tragic stories at the hospital door when I finished my shift. When I more or less broke down and went away for a weekend to have a break, a friend suggested I quit my job.

I didn't take much persuading. Instead I enrolled part-time at university and studied writing, something I *wanted* to do, rather than feeling obliged to do. This gave me energy instead of leaving me feeling helpless and inadequate as nursing had done. But that feeling that I should be working, meaning earning money, contributing, have a job, plagued me for years. Other women had families and worked, why couldn't I? Was I lazy? I hated being a "kept woman". I hated being asked "So what do you do?" at parties. I had no identity. I was just that much reviled but ultimately indispensable of women: a housewife. I couldn't talk about what I did and as much as people pay lip-service to the importance of the work women do raising a family, it isn't really valued in society, certainly not in a fiscal sense; we aren't part of the quantifiable economy.

In the early years of our marriage, Neville spent a lot of time travelling to New York for work. It was one of the hardest times in my life. We had only just moved back to Brisbane after a few years away so we had no friend network. I was alone for weeks on end, pregnant, with small children and babies. Neville called me every day and would tell me what he'd been doing. He flew first class, stayed in five star hotels, was driven around in limousines, took a helicopter flight over Manhattan, and flew to Vermont for the day. To see the Autumn leaves. I had washed nappies, taken the kids to the park, cooked dinner. It was miserable. Did anyone ever ask Paul Theroux, or Michel Peissel, or Peter Matthiessen who was looking after their children?

So I could have gone alone on the journey to Lo Manthang, (although technically only groups of two or more are allowed). Neville had already been on a trek in Nepal with a friend. But I knew it would test me and I wanted him there for support. After thirty years together, he knew me pretty well. He never tried to discourage me but would stand by ready to catch me if I fell. And anyway, I wanted to share the experience with him.

CHAPTER 3

After the Earthquake

As we waited to board the plane in Kuala Lumpur, I spotted a late-middle-aged man, with lank, greasy, grey hair, eyes wide and mouth hanging open as he gazed about him. Then he spotted us as fellow Westerners in a sea of Asians and came over.

"First time in Nepal?" he panted eagerly. We replied, no, we'd been there several times between us. He seemed to take this response as a sort of password into a club and his voice took on a conspiratorial tone.

"Where're you staying?"

"The International Guest House," I replied, realising I probably should have lied.

"Are they collecting you from the airport? Because you don't want to have to be mucking around with those taxi drivers. Of course they're supposed to use the meter but they never do. As long as you negotiate a price first."

I turned away, hoping he'd get the hint.

"Because some of them'll try and charge you 2000 rupees, and when you refuse, they'll make a scene," he persisted.

"They're normally happy with about 500 rupees," offered Neville.

"What's your hotel like? Full of internationals I suppose. How much does it cost to stay there?" he continued without giving us time to answer. "So you just get to Kathmandu and get away again as quickly as you can, like me?"

We both shook our heads and looked away.

"We'll see a lot more poverty this time," he went on. "They'll be more stressed."

He was talking about the earthquake that had occurred just five months before, killing almost 9000 people and rendering many more injured and homeless.

I was irritated with this man and his "us and them" attitude. "Them" had burrowed under my skin during my first time in Nepal. I worked at a centre for disabled children while Neville and our three sons worked at a school. My placement was chosen for me because of my previous experience as a paediatric nurse, but although I had nursed children in Australia whose health and family circumstances were heartbreaking, I wasn't prepared for the third-world conditions I found myself in, and the lack of everything. Which was kind of the point of the exercise; it was supposed to be difficult, an eye-opener for us all.

I dissolved into tears at the end of the first week when, on top of these children who would never receive adequate medical care, I watched a skeletal dog, painstakingly drag itself to its feet, stagger with stiff limbs a few steps before collapsing again. Despite being surrounded by people, this dog would starve to death and there was nothing I could do about it.

Three years later, I returned with a friend and spent another two weeks working at the same place. A severely disabled boy called Jay had come to the centre since my first visit. His mother, Sunita, lived in and worked as the cleaner and security guard in exchange for Jay being allowed to attend the centre and access what limited therapies they offered. I was told he had cerebral palsy, but in the small black and white photos Sunita showed me, two-year-old Jay stood upright next to his younger sister, smiling. The boy I met lay on the floor, brown skin stretched across his twisted skeleton, head thrown back and nostrils flared in a constant effort to breathe. He no longer smiled. While his sister Gita sat staring on, expressionless and bored, and the youngest, Sita cavorted and smiled sweetly to gain our attention, their mother held, massaged, turned, fed and cleaned up her only son, only leaving him to do her chores before returning to once more take him in her arms.

When I came in on the second Monday, I found Jay as usual propped up against his mother, but his whole body heaved with the effort of breathing, his head back, neck straining, nostrils flared, as though he was trying to reach up to air he thought maybe easier to breathe. His skin was dusky. Through Sabina, one of the staff who spoke English, Sunita told me he hadn't eaten for three days. I pressed a stethoscope to his ribcage; it sounded like a fish tank filter. It was full of the milky mush his mother spooned into him. He couldn't swallow properly, he needed a feeding tube. He needed a lot of things he could never have.

"He needs to go to hospital," I told them.

A short conversation in Nepali followed, then Sabina turned to me.

"She says she'll take him tomorrow if he's still sick."

"No, he needs to go now," I replied.

Another conversation followed then Sabina left without another word. So I left too. I couldn't stand and watch this boy die in front of me. There was nothing more I could do to help.

Three hours later Sabina turned up at our house.

e Sunita take Jay to hospital. Will you come and support them?"

We found him on a bare plastic mattress in the chaos of the emergency department at Patan hospital. Sunita had made a pillow out of a plastic bag stuffed with clothes. Jay groaned, arching his back while his mother stood grasping and rubbing his contracted hand, tears running down her face. He was admitted with severe pneumonia.

I visited Jay in hospital twice before I had to leave. Both times I begged the staff to give the boy pain relief but they dismissed me, pointing to the oxygen prongs in his nostrils. He was wracked with spasms and in terrible distress. And I knew if he recovered from the pneumonia this time, it would be only to go home and have more mush fed into his lungs. I had insisted on Jay being taken to hospital in the expectation he would be cared for palliatively, but I was operating on first-world medical expectations; in Australia, children with life-limiting conditions at the end of all treatment options were at least afforded as comfortable a death as possible, usually with morphine to smooth their passage. Narcotics, I was told by one officious doctor, would suppress Jay's already difficult breathing. No shit? So instead he was to be propped up and kept alive to suffer a bit longer.

Before I said goodbye I felt a sudden need to give Sunita something. I reached up and undid the chain hanging around my neck. On it hung a small holy medal, given to me by a lovely old nun when, at the age of eight, I lay in hospital recovering from a tonsillectomy. Feeling a little embarrassed, I fastened it around Sunita's neck and she laughed. As I embraced her, leaving her at the hospital with her dying son, I felt like I had bullied them into coming to hospital only to abandon her to fly home to my comfortable life and healthy sons.

I arrived home angry at a stupid country that couldn't care for its own children, couldn't establish a stable, uncorrupt government, couldn't even keep the lights on for more than a few hours a day, and angry at myself for my misguided interference knowing all I had done was prolong Jay's suffering.

And yet, here I was again, but this time I was not coming to try and help anyone. I was going on my own journey.

The greasy-haired man eventually gave up on us and we next spied him sitting next to another westerner. I heard him say, "Yes, this is my tenth time."

✳ ✳ ✳

About an hour after we arrived at our hotel in Kathmandu we received a message that someone was waiting in the foyer for us. We found a short and compact man dressed in a short-sleeved colourful shirt, over which he wore a vest made from suit material. He had a round happy face. This was our guide Pradeep.

After the introductions were made, Neville suggested we sit out in the garden and have something to drink. Pradeep opted for a Coke, while Neville and I drank Nepali tea.

Pradeep told us he was from a village near Namche Bazaar northwest of Kathmandu. He lived some of the time in Kathmandu where he shared a house with his son and his family, but spent three months of the year, the European summer, working in France as a cook at a hotel in the mountains. In the winter he returned to Nepal to work as a guide. When he could, he returned to his village where his wife and his mother lived. Such is the life of many Nepalese.

He hadn't been to Mustang since 2001, back when there were few lodges so they had to camp and take a lot more equipment, and when a government official had to accompany all trekking groups, and the guide had to pay for all the official's expenses. It was not a popular destination with these officials, Pradeep told us, being long and difficult, and they would often feign altitude sickness to get out of continuing the journey. He told us he'd be back early on Friday morning with a driver to take us to Pokhara, and we said goodbye.

※ ※ ※

We walked out before breakfast next morning to see Kathmandu waking up and see for ourselves what damage the earthquake had done. It was warm, and in the haze that sits permanently over Kathmandu was the familiar smell of smoke and spices. Immaculately dressed children hurried to school, stopping briefly at street-side shrines to ring the bell that wakes the sleeping god and make their equivalent of the Catholic sign of the cross: touching forehead then heart, back and forth. Women stood outside their front doors and placed rice, flower petals, and vermillion powder on the ground and sprinkled water, murmuring prayers.

There were a lot of buildings in disrepair, but then there often are in Kathmandu.

"Doesn't really look much different does it," said Neville, as we stood staring at a pile of rubble in between two buildings.

It was only when we reached Durbar Square, the original home of the Kathmandu kings, where the ancient temples were, that we saw the extent of the devastation. At least two were completely gone; hundreds of years old, they had simply crumbled to dust. The old palace, with its white plaster, Greek columns, and Union Jack balustrades from the days of Nepal's association with Britain through the East India Company, was cracked and broken and surrounded by scaffolding.

The Kumari Ghar, home to the living goddess, a pre-pubescent girl believed to be the incarnation of the goddess Taleju until her first menstrual period (or other large loss of blood), had lengths of timber propping up the front wall. We visited the Kumari on our first trip with our sons. We assembled in the courtyard and waited for her to appear at the window, which she does at intervals during the day. Signs everywhere said it was forbidden to take photos of the goddess. A hush fell and then a girl of about six years old appeared at the window, gripping the sill and swinging back and forth as little girls do, looking very bored. She was heavily made up and dressed in red silken robes. She stayed for about a minute and then retreated to the dark interior of her palace. Then all hell broke loose. A German tourist had, despite the warnings, taken a photo of the Kumari. The official who had seen her snatched her camera from her hands and before she could stop him, deleted all of her photos. She was irate and followed the official out of the courtyard and across the square, gesticulating and yelling.

In the open area where people set up market stalls, but which at that hour was still empty, I saw a dog limping along, its right front paw hanging limp and swollen. Two people beckoned to it and it sat itself down carefully between them. I couldn't help myself; I walked over and crouched down.

"His leg looks broken," I said and gently patted the poor, shivering creature. They nodded, looking sad.

I thought of my father. I often thought of him when I was travelling, especially when I saw street dogs, sick or injured. I wished I had him there to tell me what was wrong, what could be done. Dad was always curious about the world. If he saw something interesting in the street he would go up and ask someone about it. I knew how much he would have loved to be able to travel to a place like this, but Mum always poured cold water on such trips, thinking up all the things that could go wrong. After he retired, Dad booked himself a flight down to Antarctica, one of those flights where you fly along the coastline, just to see it. Mum didn't want to go and told me she thought it was a stupid thing to do.

"What a waste of money," she said. They had plenty of money for such things. About my own travels she was no less scathing, remarking when I announced my third trip to Nepal, "When are you going to get over going to these countries?"

My mother was well-read and interested in many things. She loved music and art. When I was young she used to paint. She used to drag me along to outdoor painting groups where people gathered to paint the same view. I remember becoming bored and whiny, being of pre-school age. Perhaps that's why my mother gave it up. For her seventieth birthday, maybe as a way of apologising for putting an end to her artistic career, I gave my mother a set of oil paints that had cost me a considerable sum. She looked at them and said, "What? Did you think I could spend my dotage sitting and painting?" She never used them.

My father, on the other hand used to play with me sometimes and take me on his calls when Mum wanted to go shopping. I stood in cow-sheds and watched him arm-deep in cow's backsides. I held dogs for him while he calmly put them down. I watched him pull calves out of their bellowing mothers. I used to climb into bed with him and lie there while he did the crossword before going to sleep. Sometimes the phone rang at that time and he would haul himself out of bed swearing and slamming doors to drive out to some farm miles from home. On the occasions he arrived home before dinner, I would run out to meet him. But he didn't make food the right way. He cut my sandwiches the wrong shape and once put an ice cube in my cup of tea to cool it down when there was no milk left. I can still feel the visceral horror of seeing that ice cube floating in my tea. To my father's bewilderment and, no doubt, frustration, I became an hysterical mess and refused to drink the tea. Mum would never have done such a thing. She would have made sure there was milk.

I wonder whether my mother's cast-iron, unfailing stalwartness and determination to keep calm and carry on, and my father's dedication to work (he was available 365 days a year) was the anchor to that home; I could always rely on her and Dad to be there and keep things the same.

I stood up after patting the dog and walked away. There was nothing any of us could do, which is exactly what my father would have told me.

※ ※ ※

On our way back to the hotel, I stopped in at the Seeing Hands Clinic to make an appointment for a massage. In the waiting area, three men sat, stirring to life as I entered. One of them welcomed me and I told him I would like to make a booking.

"Unfortunately, all of our female masseurs are on vacation," he said, "but we are happy to give you a massage if you are comfortable with a man."

"I don't mind," I said.

I'm quite happy to get my clothes off in front of people, probably because as a nurse I dealt with so many naked bodies that they've lost all mystery, mine included, but it really wasn't a problem here: all the masseurs were blind. The Seeing Hands Clinic was set up to train and employ people who would otherwise have no way of earning a living. He indicated a white board calendar on the wall and told me to write my name at the time I would like to come. The calendar was completely empty. There were few tourists in Kathmandu since the earthquake. I chose a time and wrote my name, wondering what was the point, especially since they couldn't see it.

I returned at the time I'd written, to find the three of them still sitting there. Mine was still the only name on the calendar. My masseur led me up a flight of stairs to a room with two tables. He told me his name was Nishan.

"Have you been blind since birth?" I asked him, as he rubbed oil into my back.

"Yes. All of us are, except one of the female masseurs. She went blind after she caught typhoid."

I asked Nishan about the earthquake and he told me he and his family lost their home. They were now living in a tin shed. He didn't know when they would afford to rebuild. I asked him how a blind person negotiates the chaos of Kathmandu, with its frantic, disorganised traffic and uneven sidewalks, given that it was hard enough for a sighted person. "Is difficult," he said, laughing.

"What do you think of the new constitution?" Seven years after the abolition of the monarchy, the government, which had changed prime ministers on a roughly yearly basis, was finally going to hand down the first constitution

"We have laws that exist on paper," he said, "but there is so much corruption."

The room was warm and a bit stuffy, and as sweat mixed with the oil I knew I would have to shower it all off as soon as I got back to the hotel—shower in water that smelt slightly metallic and ran brown, that may or may not be hot. This unreliability, from the hot water to the government, was kind of what attracted us to Nepal. Neville especially loved the fifth and chaos and the lack of over-regulation. If it was up to him we would have stayed in the cheapest, nastiest hotel in Kathmandu, without hot water and with sheets of unknown cleanliness. He just didn't care.

Our hotel, the International Guest House, was clean and comfortable but hardly luxurious. I liked the fact that what we experienced in Nepal was "real" in the sense that nothing was hidden behind that veneer of perfection found at luxury hotels. Our beds were spine-correctingly firm; the towels were clean but grey; the breakfast eggs might be raw or like rubber; and even if we got a TV or air-conditioner in our room, they both depended on whether the electricity happened to be on. Even so I kidded myself; it took a lot of energy to live with uncertainty. The stray dogs and their broken legs, the disabled kids, the knowledge that in the event of an accident there was no calling triple zero, all wore me down after a while. I took a deep breath in before I stepped out of the plane, and only let it out, in almost a sob of gratitude for having survived, when I boarded the plane to go home. Nepal was great as long as I could leave.

Back at our hotel, the owner, Mr. Gurung, was in his usual position, sitting out on the verandah that overlooked the neatly kept courtyard lawn, in his shorts and thongs, having a smoke. We got chatting to him and told him we'd walked over to Durbar Square and seen the destruction.

"What do think will happen with the temples?" asked Neville. "Do you think they'll be rebuilt?"

Mr. Gurung shrugged his shoulders. "For years the government has been over-charging tourists to visit the Durbar Square and the money was supposed to go towards maintaining the temples, but none of it has, so when the earthquake hits everything is crumbling," he told us.

CHAPTER 4

To Pokhara

Pradeep turned up with a very smart car and driver early next morning and we set off for the drive to Pokhara. Michel Peissel flew to Pokhara, there being no road between there and Kathmandu in 1964. Peissel's journey was, of course, a much greater expedition than ours. He had great difficulty finding staff, since no one was willing to travel to such a remote, unknown, and, at that time, dangerous place; Khampa guerrillas were fighting the Chinese invaders across the border in Tibet and they were reputed to rob and kill travellers in the area. A man named Calay, who had accompanied Peissel on previous expeditions agreed to go with him as his cook and servant. Another man, Tashi, whom he had befriended during the six months he had spent in Kathmandu waiting for permission, agreed to accompany him. And so he set off for Pokhara one morning with just these two and all of the food and equipment they would need for three months, in the hope that he would be able to find more men willing to join him on the expedition.

When we set out, the Tij festival was in full swing and Kathmandu was awash with women dressed in bright red saris. On the way from the airport to our hotel we had passed Pashupatinath, the Hindu shrine where bodies are cremated around the clock. A long line of red stretched from the gates up to the street where more red saris were heading in the same direction like a magnet was drawing all things red to itself. As we now headed up out of the Kathmandu Valley we passed large groups of women sitting together along the road, sharing out food and flowers. Other groups huddled together singing and dancing. Pradeep told us that the women fast and pray and take offerings to the temples for their husband's health and prosperity.

"The women do this for the men," he said, "but the men don't do this for the women." And he laughed his high-pitched giggle.

Also celebrated in the northern states of India, Tij is a festival for Hindu women to gather and celebrate their womanhood, but also for unmarried women to pray they will be granted their ideal husband and for married women to pray for their husbands. It recalls the union of Lord Shiva and his wife Parvati. On the first day the women gather for singing, dancing and feasting. From midnight they fast. On that second day they go to the temple to worship the god Shiva and place offerings. The next morning they perform a ritual purification, or puja, ceremony and after this they can eat. The next day they bathe after which they are absolved of all their sins.

As we wound up out of the valley, weaving and beeping past and between trucks and buses on tight bends, high above the rushing river below, the dingy, broken houses and the chaos of Kathmandu gave way to lush countryside. Vivid green rice paddies rose in terraces above the river and high up amongst them I spied a lone figure in brilliant red strolling along. It was becoming hot and humid and as I watched the outside temperature indicator in the car climb to thirty degrees, and noted that the car did have air-conditioning, wondered why it wasn't on. We both felt reluctant to ask. I had lived with my host family on two occasions, one in the middle of winter with no heating, and I had seen children arrive at the disabled centre all rugged up in the pre-monsoon humidity, so I knew the Nepalese were more immune to extremes of temperature. The Nepalese also never directly say no. I thought perhaps the driver was trying to conserve fuel. I didn't want him to put on the aircon because he couldn't say no, but I also didn't want to sit in a sauna for another five hours. To our relief, after a morning tea stop, Pradeep suggested we put the aircon on because it was getting a bit hot. We thanked him sincerely and drew up our windows. To travel in a private vehicle in air-conditioned comfort in Nepal was pure luxury and we enjoyed it while we could.

And so after travelling in style through the lush, post-monsoon fields, and above the raging Trisuli river, we drove into Pokhara, and along the beautiful Fewa Tal, a large lake, before turning up a short laneway to our hotel. My sybaritic heart stilled at the sight of such luxury. For one night we would be able to lie in air-conditioned comfort and watch television and even take cold drinks from the bar fridge, then shower in a pristine ensuite and dry ourselves with white fluffy towels. But of course, the power was out, so we went out for a walk.

Pokhara felt like a beachside holiday town, at least by the lake. High, dark-green hills rose sheer from the water's edge on the opposite bank, the over-hanging foliage creating shaded recesses, dark and secret. Rainbow-coloured boats sat bobbing at the waters edge waiting for hire, while Tibetans from the local refugee community pressed us to buy their beads and posters. A large police presence congregated at the gated entry to a large property. There were no signs on the high brick fence that surrounded it. The fence stretched for several hundred metres along the road side and down to the water's edge. They seemed approachable enough so I stopped and asked one of the police what this was.

"Is the summer residence of the former royal family, but now is closed," he replied.

"What will happen to it?"

"Maybe it will become a museum."

The palace in Kathmandu was turned into a museum in 2010, shortly before our first visit. A rather harsh, soviet looking building, its peeling wallpaper, stray brocade threads, worn velvet, unravelling plastic garden furniture, and overgrown greenhouse made it look more abandoned house than museum. Around the back, the buildings where the royal massacre took place in 2001 had been demolished. Crown Prince Dipendra had gone on a (supposedly drunken) rampage killing ten members of the family, including his parents, both of his siblings, and himself. Many Nepalese, still faithful to their monarch, don't believe it possible that Prince Dipendra was responsible. The Nepalese king was regarded as a divinity. Prince Dipendra lay in a coma for several days after killing his family, meaning he was briefly king. This meant he was now divine. How could a divine being be responsible for murdering their family?

When we were living with our host family I asked our host mother about the massacre.

"The phone rang about midnight. It was my father, and he told me the royal family had been murdered. We were all crying."

"Why would the Prince want to kill his family?" I asked.

"His parents wouldn't allow him to marry the girl he was in love with."

This is just one of the theories, but many more abound. One of the most popular is that the King's brother, Gyanendra who ascended the throne after Dipendra's three-day reign, was responsible. He was very unpopular, as was his son Paras.

"He thinks he's a gangster," our host father told me.

Paras had been in trouble on numerous occasions, once for allegedly running over and killing the popular Nepalese singer, Praveen Gurung. He was never charged. During our first visit to Nepal, he was staying at a resort in Chitwan National Park when he pulled out his gun and shot it in the air. He was subsequently arrested for drug offences in Thailand where he went to live.

Of the ex-queen, Komal, our host mother was scathing. "She's fat because she eats too many chocolates."

At the former palace in Kathmandu markers had been placed where each family member had fallen, one on the remaining stairs where Queen

Aishwarya had half her head blown away as she tried to flee. Bullet-holes still freckled the back concrete wall, and the smashed glass in the back door had not been replaced.

We decided to hire one of the boats and, while I lay back like a femme fatale, Neville manned the oars and rowed up past the former Royal residence. A modest two-story brick house could be seen through the trees, sitting empty. Another building sat out over the edge of the lake, the screens enclosing its verandah filthy and torn.

From the centre of the lake smoke rose and bells could be heard from the Tal Bahari Temple that sits on a small island. Pilgrims paddled out to the island where they lit butter lamps and made offerings to the goddess Bahari, watched over by the Annapurna mountains, looming above the valley and reflected in its lake. There was no motorised craft on the water to disturb the languid tranquility and I lay back and luxuriated while we drifted along.

As the sun set we sat back on our balcony, sipped our beer and cocktails, and watched the great Machhupachare, the "fishtail" mountain, turn from crystal white to hazy pink then purple. The waiter told us it is also called "tiger mountain" and pointed out the sharp ears, snout, mouth, and front paws of a crouching tiger.

Once it was dark we set out to enjoy a last good meal before we would have to endure twelve days of a bland trekking menu: rice, bread, eggs, and potato with much the same toppings of cheese and tomato paste and few fresh vegetables. Restaurants lined the street that ran along the lake called things like "Benign Restaurant" or "Typical Restaurant". Eager waiters in black pants and immaculate white shirts called to us to "just look" at their menus. We decided on a very new place, a hotel that was still being finished, where the staff were extremely eager to make a good impression, rushing to help us as soon as we made any movement and repeatedly asking if everything was ok.

"Why are there so many police in Pokhara?" I asked them as they stood around us eager to help.

They looked at each other nervously. One boy tried to explain but his lack of vocabulary on such a subject failed him. Something to do with strikes was all I could gather.

We savoured our last taste of meat and toasted our upcoming journey with good wine before wandering back through the humid night air to our hotel. Many shops were still open, their owners trying to entice us in. Here too tourist numbers were down since the April earthquake and there was an air of quiet desperation.

CHAPTER 5

Jomsom

Morning flights between Pokhara and Jomsom are always a precarious thing; they depend entirely on the weather. Too windy or foggy and there are no flights. And planes can only fly in the morning because the fierce wind from the south comes up around midday making flying too dangerous. This wind is notorious. Hot air from the Indian plains to the south rises and flows north, intensifying as it is funnelled through the Kali Gandaki canyon that cuts between the Dhaulagiri and Annapurna ranges.

In order to maximise our chances Pradeep got us to the airport by 5.30am and we sat clutching the breakfast boxes made up by our hotel—hard-boiled eggs, a cheese sandwich, a small banana, an apple and a small bottle of sickly sweet "Frooti" fruit drink—waiting to see if we'd be flying that day. It was a clear morning so our chances looked good. As we sat waiting we noticed a short, thin man of about forty, wearing baggy suit pants, helping Pradeep tag and weigh the baggage. When Pradeep came over Neville asked,

"Is that man coming with us?"

"Ahh..no," Pradeep replied.

I turned to look at the mountains changing colour as the sun rose, pink then gold and finally crystal white. A group of Indians entered the terminal and a lady in a red sari sat down near me smiling warmly. She was eager to engage me in conversation but her English was equal to my Hindi. Nevertheless, she chattered and kept gesturing towards the window where I'd been watching the mountains. I thought she was showing me how beautiful they were and I nodded, smiling. She chattered on and started making hand gestures, seeming to mimic a plane flying, but then she turned her hand upside down. I wondered whether she was warning me that as lovely as it would be to soon be flying in a plane next to those mountains, sometimes planes crashed into them. Two weeks after Neville took the same flight a couple of years before, the plane crashed into the mountain near the Jomsom airport, killing nearly everyone on board. I smiled at her and told myself what I always tell myself when flying internally in Nepal: most of them don't crash.

We had just bought scalding hot milk tea when we were called to board. We trouped out onto the tarmac into the still early morning light. Low clouds ringed the valley. It already felt humid. After the flight attendant handed out hard sweets and cotton wool balls for our ears, we roared off the airstrip and were soon above Pokhara. As I looked down on the Seti river snaking along below us, I wondered if they would ever find the American girl who had been murdered in Pokhara just a few weeks before. She had gone to Nepal alone to help with the earthquake recovery, a twenty-three year old teacher from Austin. She found accommodation in Pokhara via a couch-surfing website. The man she was staying with bashed her to death with a hammer to get her money and her iPhone. He had broken down and confessed and told police he had thrown her dismembered body into the river before he was hospitalised.

We had not long begun flying along the Kali Gandaki gorge between the Dhaulagiri and Annapurna ranges when the plane sounded like it was losing altitude. "Most of them don't crash," I reminded myself, but realised that being a flight of less than twenty minutes we were already making our descent. We landed in Jomsom and emerged into cool dry mountain air.

The same short, thin man helped carry our bags out to where a policeman sat at a desk filling in an exercise book ruled with columns.

"So, this man is coming with us on the trek?" Neville asked Pradeep again.

"Yes," Pradeep replied.

"What's his name?"

"Dipak."

Dipak was our assistant guide. He fetched and carried and generally took care of the practicalities of trekking. He was almost unfailingly good-humoured and nothing seemed to tire him. His small, thin frame belied his strength and stamina. He could neither read nor write, but the money he earned from trekking enabled him to put his children through school. He was from the same village as Pradeep and they had known each other their whole lives.

Each guide had to tell how many people they were taking into Mustang and which country they were from. I noticed there were three from Russia and guessed they were the two women and one very large man who had been on the plane with us. He was carrying a large camera and looked like an excited school boy, with round rosy cheeks and a frame that he could barely fit into the narrow plane seat.

Once the official business was done Pradeep took us to the Monalisha (sic) Guest House just along from the airport and we sat in the warm, sunny dining room upstairs, ate our breakfast box and drank milk tea. We were still waiting for our horses to arrive so when I'd finished eating I went outside to check out Jomsom.

As I stood in the street outside the lodge and looked up and down the cobbled street I realised that at last I was on my way to Lo Manthang. I remembered the postcard of Mustang pinned to the cork board in my office at home, which I had bought partly to inspire me to get to Lo Manthang, partly as that magic that is supposed to occur if you put pictures of the things you want where you'll constantly see them. It showed red, white and grey pointed chortens reaching above fluted yellow cliffs and, further back, cloud-wreathed Himalayas. Just looking at that picture you could sense the clear air and imperial silence that must permeate that ancient land.

My therapist and I had struggled to work out why I would miss a home in which I was never really happy. She suggested various theories, but in the end, I realised it boiled down to its seeming permanence. "It was always there," I told her. And that, we decided was the thing. It may not have been happy, but it was reliable for the fact that nothing ever changed. I could always retreat to that place where everything was certain and routine.

But now my childhood home was gone, and I had sent myself into completely the opposite state. I was heading into one of the most remote, inaccessible, and immutable places on Earth. Me, who couldn't walk for more than half an hour without tiring and had had six horse-riding lessons. I had been the instigator of a trip that had involved the recruitment of two guides, and a horse, as though I was some kind of resilient, fearless adventurer. What if I couldn't keep up the pace?

It was still only about seven in the morning and the town was just waking up. Nilgiri loomed high above, its white peak glistening in the early morning light. It was whisper quiet. Except for the occasional truck wheezing along the street, the whole place was filled with a serene silence. The tropical humidity of Pokhara had been busy with noise: the high police presence, the Tibetan refugees trying to sell their beads and posters, the shop-keepers all but begging you to come into their shops, new hotels under construction. But here in Jomsom, at least this early in the morning, it was still. Long shadows fell across the cobbles and smoke rose from chimneys.

I walked across the street to a small shop to buy some tissues, feeling slightly guilty about this. A guidebook from 2009 stated:

> At the conclusion of the trek you are required to register again with the ACAP [Annapurna Conservation Area Project] office and show all your rubbish to prove you have carried it out for disposal in Jomsom.

I'd heard nothing about this mentioned and suspected that if it were ever enforced, it wasn't now. Nevertheless, I was acutely conscious of taking anything disposable into Mustang. But I still bought those tissues.

About nine o'clock two horses were brought to the entrance of the lodge by a boy with a mop of dyed orange hair on the top of his head with the sides his natural dark brown colour closely shaved. He had a silver tusk-shaped earring in his left ear. He wore a blue zip-up jacket and black jeans, fraying at the bottoms and low-slung to reveal the top of his Calvin Klein underpants. He wore worn-out joggers and no socks. He smiled shyly and tossed his head with indifference when introduced to us. This was Abhinav, a seventeen-year-old boy who lived in Jomsom and who would be accompanying us to care for the horses.

We had tried to talk our youngest son, Tom, into coming on the trip. He was also seventeen and in his final year of school. We told him it was a rare chance to see an unusual, remote part of the world, all paid for. But he got his drivers' license a couple of months before we went and the thought of a month parent-free and being able to drive anywhere, outweighed any opportunity to see some dusty old Nepalese village in the middle of nowhere. I wondered now how he and Abhinav would have got on.

Before we left for Nepal, I worried about leaving Tom, not so much because I thought at seventeen he wouldn't be okay—we had plenty of friends to look out for him, he spent some time with his grandparents, and his two brothers were there—more that I felt a bit guilty, leaving him to go on holiday for four weeks. But then, this never stopped my own parents. When I was eight, they left me with the people who lived up behind our house in Bellingen, to go on a trip to Europe. They were people my parents had known for years, but they didn't socialise with them, so they weren't really friends. They knew them from our church and my sisters went to school with their two girls. The family were kind to me and very accommodating to my parents when they decided to extend their trip from two months to three. At the time, it seemed to me like a bit of an adventure, but after I became a parent myself, the thought of leaving my eight-year-old child with the neighbours to go somewhere for three months was impossible to imagine.

All the horses I saw in Mustang had a simple saddle, which, as well as being held in place by the girth strap, had a piece that looped around the base of the tail. The saddle sat on a blanket plus a piece of carpet, and on top of all this was placed a cushion or pillow and then another piece of carpet. My horse's blanket was frayed around the edges and the canvas and leather straps were similarly worn. The other horse was loaded up with our packs which had been put into old plastic feed bags and then tied onto the saddle. I thought both horses looked thin and in poor condition, but my knowledge of horses being pretty much limited to those six lessons, and these being different horses altogether, I wasn't sure. They were smaller than the horses you see in Australia and where ours are usually sleek and shiny, these had woolly coats. Like all horses in Mustang they each wore a bell which clear ringing would float on the air and accompany us on the journey.

When they were ready I was asked whether I wanted to walk the first bit out of town, or ride straight away. I was keen to see if all those lessons were going to pay off so I decided to ride. Both Dipak and Abhinav helped me to mount and did so every time I got on or off the horse. I don't know whether it was because I was female, obviously incompetent, or they do it for everyone, but if I decided I was mounting or dismounting they would always rush up to help me. And of course I had to wear my helmet. Abhinav looked at me like there was something wrong with me when I pulled this on over my bucket hat. It looked ridiculous, but I wanted to avoid both sunburn and a head injury. He glanced over at Dipak with an ironic look.

"Helmet," said Dipak and laughed good-naturedly.

CHAPTER 6

Kagbeni

As we walked through the waking town people stared. Maybe they stared at all horse-going foreign trekkers, or maybe it was the helmet. And now we were out of town and heading along the great Kali Gandaki river. The gravel and stones on the narrow path became slippery under the horses' hooves, which were unshod, and Dipak told me to dismount. The river bed was very wide, but only fairly small rivulets ran through it. We were in Autumn, when the river is at its lowest. In Spring, melting snow and glacial melt-water swell the river. Its grey stones stretched between towering cliffs. We followed the river until we came up against a sheer spur that protruded into the river bed. Here the river was running fast and deep. Pradeep decided to go up onto the road above. I was told to get back on the horse and Abhinav, first removing his old shoes, took my reins and led me through the water to a bank of gravel. The horse was reluctant to enter the water, but by pulling and yelling sternly at the poor beast he got it to move. He then led me back over again on the other side of the spur. He indicated for me to dismount then pulled the horse back into the water and around to where Neville was waiting. Meanwhile, Dipak had taken off his boots, rolled up his pants and begun wading across and around, laughing and waving his arms as though the water wasn't freezing cold. Then Neville got on the horse and Abhinav led him across, reins in one hand, Neville's walking poles in the other. It dawned on me for the first time, that these were now our "staff". Never in a million years would Neville or I have been expected to wade across as Dipak had done. I felt like an old-fashioned memsahib as I rode along and everyone stood ready to do my bidding eagerly and with diligence.

Which was lovely and romantic on the face of it, but after a while I got the distinct impression these three men regarded me as weak and doomed to fail.

This was a short day as we were only going as far as Kagbeni. We stopped at a very small village called Ekla Batti, really just a couple of lodges and a shop, and swapped the bags onto the brown horse that I'd been riding. It had been a little hard to control, so the brown one took the bags and I mounted the white one instead. Then with Abhinav shouting "La! La!" and making squeaking and singing noises to get the horses moving, we set off again. Pradeep predicted that the wind would start to come up about 10.30 and like clockwork the breeze came up and continued to strengthen as the morning wore on. By lunch time we were in Kagbeni and the wind was whipping the prayer flags tied to poles and shaking the apple trees. Our home for the night was the Nilgiri View Lodge and our room did have a wonderful view of the mountain. The wind battered and whistled at our windows and moaned around the building. We were the only guests.

I confess to being relieved at travelling only three hours that day. I knew the subsequent days would be longer and although I would be sitting on a horse for much of it, it was still an effort. It's not as though I could put my head down and have a snooze like when you're travelling in a vehicle. And yet I wanted to see this landscape, this extraordinary place. I was now being forced to reconcile the idea of seeing Mustang with the reality.

After giving our lunch order to Dipak, Neville and I, left alone in the dining room, looked out across the village. The sun streamed through the windows where swarms of black flies buzzed and butted against the glass. Neville smiled at me.

"How are you feeling?" he asked.

"Fine," I replied. "Glad it's a short day."

He laughed. "So you're a horse rider now?"

"Mm, not a very good one."

"So you don't think you'll take up horse-riding when you get home?"

"I doubt it. But at least I don't have to walk."

"No, walking's good!"

We gazed out across the flat rooftops and walled gardens to the far bank of the river and the snow-capped mountains. We had made it to the start of our adventure. I had survived thus far. I knew the coming days would be more demanding, longer time on the horse, climbing to higher altitude. I has never been at altitude so had no idea how it might affect me. Neville told me he had had trouble sleeping when he reached above four thousand metres when he trekked the Annapurna circuit two years before. But he said a younger woman travelling with her brother who, when she developed a strong headache and trouble breathing, had no choice but to descend immediately, even though it was ten o'clock at night, lest she risk dying on the mountain.

Altitude sickness is strange in that it tends to affect younger, fitter people more than older and less fit people, which seems peculiarly unfair. But I was both middle-aged and relatively unfit, so I had that much going for me. Nothing ever seemed to affect Neville, neither fatigue, food, or place. He would happily live in a box and put the same clothes on every day. Indeed, while I stand with the fridge door open each morning agonising over what to eat for breakfast, he will happily eat cereal and vegemite toast every single morning. He can eat anything and sleep anywhere.

※ ※ ※

We lunched on dal bhat (lentils and rice) and apple fritters (although on the menu they were spelled variously "filders", "filters" or "filtres") drizzled with honey, washed down with milky coffee. Then Pradeep reappeared.

"We can go now and see the monastery, I think so," he said.

We folded our arms tight and bowed our heads against the wind as we followed Pradeep down a path to a large chorten. Chortens, or stupas, are religious monuments, squat like a buddha meditating. They contain objects of spiritual value, often relics of holy monks, and are believed to bring good karma, which is why they are often found at the entrance to villages. This one marked what would have been the original entrance to Kagbeni. Stooping to enter, once inside we could stand straight. Brilliantly coloured thangkas, traditional religious paintings, lined the walls, depicting gods seated amongst curling leaves and flowers, bowls of fruit at their feet. Below them was swirling water, while above them blue skies with white, fluffy clouds. Directly overhead was one large mandala, surrounded by brilliant lapis lazuli blue and twelve smaller mandalas. All was covered with chicken wire, and a photo of the Dalai Lama and Sakya Trinzin, head of the Sakya sect of Tibetan buddhism, had been tucked under the wire in one corner.

Michel Peissel describes Kagbeni as a "Tibetan-style fortress town" and we now entered the old part of the village where the houses joined together in one stuccoed fortification. The straw and manure-strewn pathway became narrower and darker as it squeezed between white walls and ducked under parts of houses. The smell of manure and urine permeated the village, and indeed every village we came to. Calves wandered about mooing as though calling for their mothers. The odd chicken pecked about, turning left then right in panic as we approached. Old women sat in doorways turning prayer beads through work-worn fingers. They looked as though coated in years of dirt, their hair matted and stiff, and they smiled tired, toothless smiles and nodded to us. Small, grubby children smiled and called "Namaste".

We followed Pradeep as he hurried on, closely followed by Dipak, who strolled more sedately, hands clasped behind his back, and entered a courtyard, where young monks ran streaming out of a large, red, square building. This was the Kag Chode Thupten Samphel Ling monastery. It was built in 1429 and is still used today, but a new monastery was being built next to it. The earthquake had caused a large crack to zig-zag down the wall to the right of the entrance, and a piece had fallen away from the outer layer. The main assembly room, we were to discover, was like all the monasteries throughout Mustang (and indeed Tibet as we later found), dimly lit, but colourfully painted with thangkas. One gold statue of Buddha lit from above sat behind glass in the middle of the the far wall, surrounded by several smaller statues, some wrapped in orange silk katas. Seven silver bowls of water—seven pure offerings—and a lighted butter lamp stood on the shelf before them. Two rows of low seats ran along the floor facing each other and before each seat a holy book, strips of printed paper held by two wooden boards.

"Unfortunately, we cannot go onto the roof, as it is not safe," one of the monks told us. The earthquake had made the building unstable.

Outside, the young monks clustered around an adult monk who was giving out afternoon tea. They ran around like all little boys, yelling and jumping, all with heads shaved and wearing ochre robes, although one boy wore a Superman jumper over his, another a Spiderman singlet despite the cold wind. Pradeep told us it is still the tradition in Mustang that second sons are given to the monastery. Some looked as young as seven.

After giving the prayer wheels along the back wall of the monastery a spin, Pradeep and Dipak left us and we wandered on through the village alone. We passed the "Yakdonalds", its menu posted outside boasting yak cheeseburgers and fries. A grubby 7Eleven sign hung above this. The shop was closed.

We crossed a bridge made of new, clean, timber, the muddy river rushing in a torrent beneath us, and were hit by the full force of the wind. Grit blew into my eyes and stuck to the vaseline on my lips.

I had to hold my hat firmly with my hand. An elderly monk came along behind us and, laughing, pointed at the bridge. He then laughed again at the wind and continued on his way towards the small village of Tiri on the opposite bank.

When we got back to the lodge I changed into a T-shirt and felt grit fall from my long-sleeved top and when I got into bed that night there was grit in the sheets.

Each night before dinner, Pradeep and Dipak sat with us as we ate and Pradeep told us stories of his past treks and of his time working in France. Dipak sat clutching a glass of clear raksi, the local moonshine, and listened mostly as his English was not so good. Pradeep told us that as well as his two sons, who were now in their thirties, he and his wife had had a daughter, but she was born two months early and because they were in the village, far from medical help, she died.

"That must have been sad for your wife," I said.

"Err, yes, but it was a long time ago and she is ok now," he replied matter-of-factly.

I wondered how true this was. Maybe living without the sort of immediate medical help we take for granted, and seeing people die more often, makes the Nepalese more accepting of these things when they happen. A year after my first volunteering stint at the disability centre, one of the boys died after an epileptic seizure. When I wrote expressing my sorrow at this to the director, he replied,

"Yes, we are also sad, but it is the reality."

But just before I returned to Nepal the second time, I saw on Facebook that a beautiful girl of sixteen who had Down Syndrome and whom I had taught at the centre, had died. I was told her parents had taken her to hospital because she was vomiting. As the nurses struggled with her to remove her clothes she choked on her vomit. I remembered her almost crying with frustration when I failed to understand what she was asking me one day. It was only when she managed to say "little house" in English that I realised she wanted the jig-saw puzzles I had brought with me, one being of a house. At other times she sat happily looking at the pictures in a brightly illustrated Jehovah's Witness children's bible.

Her heartbroken father had her image tattooed over his heart. Years later he still posted on her Facebook page, family photos with her smiling face.

That first night Pradeep suggested we try some apple brandy, made by the lodge owners from the abundant local apples. It was sweet and warming. I chose garlic soup for dinner, recommended to mitigate the effects of altitude.

"This is good choice, I think so," Pradeep approved.

We had more apple fritters for dessert, then Pradeep and Dipak left us to have their own dinner. Always Pradeep sat with us while Dipak brought our food. Abhinav was never seen in the dining room. This, apparently, was how the hierarchy of trekking staff worked. At 8.30 we went to bed. That night I wrote in my notes:

> So, so quiet here. So peaceful. Only the sound of the wind and a small cat meowing pitifully. The wind is still up but has lost some force. So nice to go to bed early with no noise. Maybe I hear the rushing river.

CHAPTER 7

Into Restricted Territory

We woke next morning to the sound of tiny brown sparrows hopping and chirruping amongst the piles of wood stacked around the edges of the roofs on every house. This wood is very occasionally used for fuel, but it is mainly a sign of wealth as it must be brought from far away at some expense, there being few trees in Mustang. I stepped out onto the rooftop terrace outside our room and stood watching and listening as the village woke up. Still the only sounds were the birds and the rushing river and the occasional voice as people called to each other. There was the smell of smoke and the spices used for dhal: cumin, garlic, ginger, turmeric. To the south Nilgiri was covered by cloud. Across the grey muddy river, barren hills rose, dotted with stunted spiky bushes whose dull green dissolved into the grey of the surrounding rocks and, above this, a clear blue sky. On the flat ground by the river were squares of buckwheat fields. Directly below me was a kitchen garden growing spinach, cabbages and what looked like a pumpkin vine, and surrounded by apple trees laden with red fruit.

I looked across the rooftops of the village to a long white wall of prayer wheels on a flat rise above the river. One by one three women came along the wall spinning the wheels. At the end they prostrated themselves before a shrine, then turned with hands pressed together towards the river, then back again to the shrine where they prostrated themselves again. Their morning prayers done they walked off to start their day. The air was cool and fresh. I looked to the North and felt the thrill of standing on the threshold of an adventure.

This was where we entered the restricted area of Upper Mustang. There are many reasons for the restrictions and they have changed over the years. Upper Mustang is ecologically and culturally sensitive. It is an isolated, mountainous desert being located in the rain-shadow of the Himalayas and, until a rough road was completed, it was only accessible on foot or by horse and this for only part of the year. The river becomes difficult to cross in the spring, and in the winter, snow, blizzards, and the intense cold, make travelling difficult. Indeed most of the inhabitants of Upper Mustang leave in the winter, travelling to Kathmandu and India to trade. The old people and children are left behind to care for the animals. Water is scarce and many supplies, particularly for tourists, must be carried in.

It was formerly part of the area in western Tibet called Ngari, annexed by Nepal in the seventeenth century, and it retains much of its Tibetan culture. Nearly every lodge in Upper Mustang displays a large picture of Lhasa, the Tibetan capital, despite having been part of Nepal for more than three hundred years. Its religion, language and, at least for some of the women, manner of dress, is Tibetan. And while the war that was being waged across the border between the Khampa guerrillas and the Chinese when Michel Peissel travelled to Lo Manthang has long finished, Upper Mustang is still a sensitive area. The Chinese border is just twenty kilometres from Lo Manthang and easily accessible; over the years it has been a popular crossing point for Tibetan refugees. The Chinese exert a lot of pressure on the Nepalese government to stop these refugees entering the country.

Before we could leave, Pradeep had to go to the ACAP check-post to show our permits and register us. We waited outside in the sun.

A mother cow stood outside the office suckling her calf, oblivious of our presence. I looked over the railing that ran along the path above the river bank. A pile of rubbish—chip packets, soft drink cans, beer bottles, cardboard boxes and bits of plastic—lay under the bushes. According to ACAP, which was set up in 1986 to protect the environmental and cultural diversity of Upper Mustang, " ...litter, particularly the wastes produced by trekkers and hoteliers, is [a] major concern. It is estimated that an average trekking group of 15 people generates about 15 kgs of non-biodegradable and non-burnable garbage in 10 days trek, producing tons of garbage in mountain regions annually". The brochure with this information was supposed to be given to us at the start of our trek, but the office had run out of them. It says:

> Before entering Upper Mustang, your group must complete a food items checklist at the ACAP check-post at Kagbeni. On your return, the list will verify if you carry out all non-biodegradable packaging material (cans, bottles, plastics, etc.) that you brought with you. Thus, we hope to keep pollution at a minimum.

This never happened. Disposal of waste is a problem in Mustang because until packaged food from outside the area began arriving there was no such thing. Everything was used. Animal dung is still spread out to dry on roof tops and ledges along the fronts of buildings and used as fuel, there being a scarcity of wood in such a barren landscape. The only rubbish bins I ever saw were the cardboard boxes or cut down plastic jerry cans placed in the corner of the toilets for us Westerners to put our toilet paper and tissues in, something else Nepalis never use. They use water for cleaning themselves after using the toilet and blow their noses and spit phlegm onto the ground. Hence my guilt at buying tissues in Jomsom.

Being a woman, there was another contingency I had to plan for when I still thought I would have to account for all disposables taken into Mustang: my period. Traditionally in Nepal, having a period has been uncomfortable and difficult if not deadly. In a practice called Chhaupadi, women are banished from the family home for the duration of their period. They are shunned by family members, particularly men who believe if a menstruating woman even looks at them they will become sick. They are forbidden from preparing food and must use separate utensils when eating. They can't eat meat or dairy foods for fear it will make the cows sick. In very recent times women have died from exposure, suffocation and snake bite after being forced to spend the duration of their period in rough huts or animal enclosures. Here they are also at risk of sexual assault from village men.

Young girls stop going to school during their period either because of the lack of sanitation in most schools, or because they simply can't afford pads, or both. The lack of sanitary pads can mean some women resort to using dirty rags, leading to infection. Many give up school altogether as a result. Chhaupadi was banned in Nepal in 2005 but in the poorer, rural areas is still practiced.

Even in our own society menstruation is a bit like death: we don't talk about it and it's kept hidden. No one holds a pad or tampon in their hand in full view of the world as they go off to the toilet. Getting period blood on your pants or skirt is one of the most dreaded of embarrassments. There's no doubt there is still an element of yuck about it, that women are a little bit dirty. My own mother remembered her mother being unable to attend church after having a baby until she underwent a ritual of purification. Traditionally, Nepalese women were required to be purified with cow urine after their period before they could re-enter the home.

After some research I did find reusable, washable cloth pads, somewhat coyly made from colourful fabrics rather than plain white. They were washable, but not very dryable. I had visions of myself trotting along on my horse with wet pads pegged to the saddle. Being the only female in the expedition party with four other males, one of them a teenager, this was never going to do. In the end I acquired a menstrual cup. This small silicone cone-shaped cup is inserted into the vagina, it catches the blood, is then retrieved, emptied, rinsed and replaced. When not in use, mine concertinaed down to fit into a plastic container about the size of a fifty-cent piece.

And it is the menstrual cup that is being offered by NGOs to help Nepalese woman manage their period. Menstrual cups are reusable and last up to ten years, negating the need to buy pads. The other benefit of using a menstrual cup is that evidence of a period can be concealed to an extent. Every menstruating woman on the planet knows there is no foolproof method of stopping blood reaching the outside world. Periods start without much warning, pads can become saturated, blood can bypass mis-placed menstrual cups or overflow them. But the reusable pad is also being offered as an alternate not just for its sustainability, but because it provides a source of income for the women who make them. There are also issues around virginity that can cause young women to baulk at using a menstrual cup in the same way they would refuse to use a tampon.

Of course all of this reusable menstrual equipment goes a long way to preventing waste that takes hundreds of years to degrade. I calculated that in the four years during which I used a menstrual cup, I stopped approximately seven hundred and twenty pads going to landfill.

The paperwork done we headed off at last along a track beside the river. We climbed to a rise away from the river and stopped for a quick morning tea break near an organic apple farm. As there was a surfeit of apples at every village I wondered who owned it, and indeed whether all the apples in Mustang weren't "organic". I would have asked someone, but I didn't think I would have been able to make myself understood. I once tried to ask Abhinav if the horses had names.

"Khoda," he replied, mistaking the question. Khoda is Nepali for horse.

"No. What is this one's name?" I asked pointing at one of the horses.

He looked confused then said, "I don't know," and quickly got up and left.

"So you'll have been through the desert on a horse with no name," quipped Neville.

This was Neville's third trek in Nepal. He had trekked the Annapurna Circuit with a friend, and (almost) to Gokyo Lake in the Everest Region with our eldest son, Christopher and his friend Ollie, so he was a pro. He had the trekking clothes—light and breathable—the walking poles, and the boots. And I knew he would be there to get me through, or make me feel better if I couldn't go on.

I had to walk the next part because it was very steep and slippery with large, loose stones—too dangerous to ride down. Neville set off with Pradeep, and Abhinav guided the horses down while I inched my way down, feet sideways, with Dipak at my elbow ready to catch me the second I fell, which I very nearly did a couple of times. Once down, we were back on the road and had to step aside for the occasional bus or jeep. Abhinav would quickly run up and take hold of my horse's bridle and pull it aside. We stopped for lunch at a village called Chhuksang then again followed the river until we reached a steel bridge. This crossed the river where a stone tunnel had formed. Some time in the distant past the huge rock on the opposite side of the river had fallen against the other side to form this tunnel.

The photo in Michel Peissel's book shows a very primitive wooden bridge, really just planks bolted together with no side railings. The steel bridge we crossed was like a cage with concrete ramps flanked by gabion walls, but it looked like this was soon to be replaced. That afternoon we watched as a jeep sought one way and then another trying to cross the river to rejoin the road on the other side. When it is flowing swiftly this must become impossible, which is why a proper road bridge was under construction. It is ridiculous that I feel sad about this. No doubt if I lived in Mustang, far from medical or other help, anything that made the journey south faster would be welcomed.

But the sadness is not about the road, but the fear that something precious and rare will inevitably disappear from the world. With the convenience of the road comes the change that threatens the very existence of Lo Manthang. My sense that this place I had only just discovered was disappearing fast was what compelled me to see it as soon as I could. The reason to see it was vanishing. A real mediaeval walled city was in danger of become a Disneyfied tourist attraction where the centuries-old rituals, rooted in deep belief about keeping bad spirits at bay, bad influences that would threaten their crops, bring disease or destroy the Kingdom itself, would become entertainment for those threatening influences.

In 2019, four years after Mustang, we travelled to China and through Tibet. When we checked into our hotel in Beijing the front desk staff asked us what we were planning to do.

"Well, go and see the Great Wall," said Neville and I nodded. But I was nodding out of a sense of obligation. I had that feeling one must see the most advertised attractions when one has the chance. But why? A driver was arranged and day two in Beijing was going to be a trip to the Wall. But as the day before wore on, I had the sinking feeling that I would be sacrificing day two in Beijing to see something in which I had no interest. Also it involved a lot of walking and stairs.

"You don't have to come," Neville said, sensing my growing reluctance. But I felt guilty. As though I was wasting an opportunity. But then I had learnt my lesson last time I felt compelled to visit something one is expected to go and see.

On our return from Mustang, before going home, we made a brief side trip to Delhi for three days, and decided we really should go to see the Taj Mahal. Like the Eiffel Tower I couldn't care less if I never saw it, but I loathed Delhi and this would at least be a day out of it. We drove for three hours each way from Delhi to see the Taj Mahal. What the millions of photos of the Taj Mahal don't show is the squalor you have to wade through before you get to it. Agra is dirty and chaotic and you have to run the usual gauntlet of people hassling you to buy stuff. Was it worth it though, once we entered and saw the great mausoleum? Not really.

I was tired, it was thirty-seven degrees, and we had a tedious guide who droned on and on with his much rehearsed spiel. I took photos but they looked like all the other photos.

I went looking for approval for my decision to forego the Great Wall, in case I would regret it, and found it in Patrick Holland's *Riding The Trains In Japan*.

> I had first seen the Wall as a student in Beijing and been underwhelmed as one often is at famous and over-photographed sites that no longer have a use apart from their value as tourist draw cards…That day I could easily imagine that the Wall was fake– that it had been set up on the back of a legend to part tourists with their money.

I knew the city of Lo Manthang would remain, the buildings, the wall, but if the outside world could more easily come to it, and its inhabitants, particularly the younger ones, more easily leak away to the outside world, would Lo Manthang "no longer have a use"?

I had to dismount to cross the bridge then remount on the other side. We rode through some small rivulets and the horses stopped for a long drink before we again began to climb. As we trudged up the almost vertical approach to the village of Tsele I looked at the deep river gorge to our left, a tributary of the Kali Gandaki, and imagined Peissel and his yak caravan toiling up this gorge as he describes in his book. We followed a track and entered Tsele through a gateway made from thin tree trunks between two stone walls. On top of the gateway sat a box surrounded by stones inside which was a figure made from stone and wood: a talisman to ward off evil spirits.

CHAPTER 8

Tsele

We continued climbing up through the village between white-washed walls before arriving at our lodge, the only one open in Tsele although there seemed to be another three. Now we could look across at the dramatic red cliffs that had loomed high above the river crossing. High up in the face of the cliffs was a row of caves in a perfect straight line. About fifty metres off the ground these caves are believed to be thousands of years old and are among some 10,000 such caves throughout Mustang. We could still look south to Nilgiri and Tilicho but the scenery here had become more dramatic. The wind had picked up like clockwork at about 10 and now late in the afternoon groaned and howled around our lodge. We took tea on the terrace high above the village, with a red, plastic tablecloth nailed to the table, looking across to the cliffs, then set out to explore Tsele.

One old man sat alone on a step spinning a prayer wheel in his hand and bid us a weary "Namaste" as we passed. There were plots of wheat on the northern side, protected by the wind, and more apple orchards. As the sun set, women gathered whatever crop it was that had been cut, into a pile and covered it with what looked like an old plastic tent.

Below us in a small courtyard a game of volleyball was being played, triumphant, joyful cries rising into the dimming light.

At dinner that night were a small group of Germans and their Nepalese guide. I felt an unreasonable resentment towards them, wanting Lo Manthang to be my destination alone. This was of course highly petulant of me and once we got to know them a bit the feeling evaporated. The guide was the husband of one of the women and they spent half the year in Nepal and half in Germany. I asked the German woman how she found living in Nepal and whether she spoke Nepali.

"Only a few words," she said, "words for food so I can get by when I'm shopping in the market."

I displayed the few words of Nepali I had learned and my favourite phrase:

"Mati janus!"

Her husband laughed: "Go upstairs!"

Now there was no internet and no phone coverage either, although sometimes on higher ground my phone would start to ping with texts. There were no longer pedestal toilets either. Here we shared an outside squat toilet. I was quite expecting this and even welcomed the challenge, but whilst I play at being brave and adventurous, proudly embracing the discomforts of trekking—squat toilets, the lack of hot showers, bland food—the sybarite within me eventually emerges and I fantasise about lamb cutlets, fresh vegetables, soft beds and clean fresh sheets.

But that night in Tsele I had to accept that squat toilets in mostly dark, concrete cubicles would be my lot for the next ten days. This particular toilet was reached through a passageway between rooms and out behind the lodge. There was a door at the outer end of the passageway that locked from the inside. If it was left unbolted it banged in the relentless wind. I knew this may become a problem if I had to visit the toilet at night, which I inevitably did. With head-torch on I walked up the corridor and undid the bolt. There was no other way to secure it from banging than by rebolting it which I couldn't do from the outside. I suppose I could have found a rock to hold it, but I would have been searching in the dark, so instead I decided to be as quick as I could in the hope that I would beat the person who became annoyed enough by the banging to get up and bolt the door before I returned. I wasn't, and when I emerged from the toilet the door was locked. I didn't want to wake up the whole lodge banging on the door, so I tapped on what I thought was our window, whispering loudly, "Nev!". I got no response and since I wasn't even sure it was our window I didn't persist. There was nothing for it but to bang on the door until someone came.

Eventually a rather frightened-looking Nepalese man opened it.

He said, "It was open," but I'm not sure that's what he meant.

"Wasn't it bolted?" I replied, wondering if I'd made a mistake.

I must have looked angry, because he said, still looking scared, "I didn't know."

The conversation didn't make sense and I wasn't angry, just unnerved from being locked out of a lodge in the actual middle of nowhere, after using a squat toilet in a concrete bunker lit only by my feeble head-torch.

I had also begun to feel the effects of the altitude. We were at just over 3000 metres by the time we reached Tsele and I had a slight headache. This was not that unusual for me and I assumed maybe I was dehydrated or that my body was not used to sitting on a horse for hours, forgetting that I was now at a higher altitude than I'd ever been. But by the time we were unpacking for the night I'd begun to feel light-headed and generally unwell. I took something for the headache and once I'd had some dinner I felt better.

That night in the room next to the dining room, the Nepalese were glued to a TV (via a satellite dish on the roof) watching the parliament finally hand down their constitution that had been seven years and multiple changes of prime minister coming. What we didn't know then, was that this was going to cause problems for us and enormous and ongoing problems for Nepal.

CHAPTER 9

Samar

As I lay awake in the early morning light, I heard the clear ringing of the horse bells and slow plodding of hooves come up outside our window. I pulled aside the thin curtain and saw Abhinav putting a feed bag over each of the horse's heads before saddling them for the day. Apart from the occasional distant voice, the only other sound was the chirrup of the sparrows.

And so began the routine we would follow for the next ten days. Rising early, we would wash and pack before going to the dining room for breakfast. While we ate, Dipak and Abhinav would put our packs into the white plastic bags ready to be strapped onto the pack horse. That morning, like so many mornings, Abhinav was running late, causing Pradeep to eventually conclude that he was lazy. So Neville, Pradeep and I set off on foot. Dipak and Abhinav would catch up.

We followed the road out and up above Tsele. I turned to look down on the roofs of the houses, all rimmed with piles of wood, and across to the rising cliffs on the other side of the river gorge. The snowy peaks of the Annapurnas rose behind them far to the south. We were now leaving the Kali Gandaki and heading north-west through the villages of Samar, Shyangmochen, and on to Ghiling. We were also leaving the excoriating wind behind for now, but would re-meet it at Lo Manthang. We only walked a short way when Neville and Pradeep turned off the road and set off up a steep narrow track, unsuitable for the horses. So I sat on a rock and waited for the horses which I could see coming. I peered down into the deep gorge which ascends next to Tsele, the Ghyakar Khola, a tributary of the Kali Gandaki, and assumed this was the one Peissel took with his yak caravan. It was indeed narrow and steep in places and I wondered how ponderous yaks could traverse such terrain. When the horses finally arrived I rode for a short time before I had to dismount again as the path became too dangerous for riding. Now Dipak, Abhinav and I sat and waited on the edge of the gorge for Neville and Pradeep to catch up. Opposite was another village, the same white-washed houses topped with bundles of wood and surrounded by an oasis of green trees and terraced walled fields. I pointed to it and asked Abhinav the name of the village.

"Ghyakar," he replied, looking bored.

He seemed to regard me with a mixture of contempt and suspicion. He'd done this trip many times, he was carrying my day pack, he had to look after my horses and he probably wasn't being paid much to do it. We didn't know how much, since we paid Pradeep and he paid Dipak and Abhinav.

After Neville and Pradeep arrived we set off up a narrow track cut into the side of the cliff. It climbed steeply becoming stairs at times. The rock hung low overhead in places. It was hard going. It seemed like we would be climbing forever and I kept hoping that around the next bend it would level out, but it kept going up. Again, Dipak walked close behind me. He told me to go slowly.

"We have time," he said gently.

I thanked God I had chosen to ride a horse to Lo Manthang because struggling up those steps I knew I would never make it there on foot. We paused about half way up where we also caught up with the Germans from our lodge.

"Tik chha, didi?" asked the Nepalese guide, laughing at my exhaustion.

"Tik chha hoina," I replied, panting as I tried to catch my breath.

Dipak laughed at my bad Nepali. "Tik chaina," he corrected.

There were many times that day when I had to dismount because the track was too steep both going up and down, steep and with loose stones. But as we ascended, we saw the mountains to the south rising with us and it seemed we were rising above the clouds that ringed them. To the west steep barren hills rose above us, dotted everywhere with spiky, stunted bushes. Settling on top of these were forbidding clouds, dark and heavy, that in the end brought only the briefest shower of rain.

We stopped for morning tea in Samar, which name means "red earth". The horses always began to speed up as we came into a village, so relieved were they at the prospect of a break. I sympathised. A lovely grove of trees fed by a stream channelled through the village greeted us on approach. The horses stopped at the first house we came to, but Dipak indicated that we needed to cross the stream and keep going a bit further. So I continued on not realising until too late that he meant for us to cross the stream. There was a small footbridge across it, but my horse had gone past it before I realised we needed to turn. Since it always followed the brown horse which was already crossing, all I could do was hang on tight as it made a huge downward step into the stream and up onto the opposite bank, a scary moment for a beginner horse-rider.

We continued up and, with relief, I dismounted before passing through a short, low passageway lined with prayer wheels and painted in black, red, yellow and white stripes, the original gateway into the village, before stopping at the Annapurna Guest House. Here we sat at tables in the kitchen where a wood fire burned under one stove and while a young woman dressed in traditional Tibetan clothes made us milk tea on a gas cooker, tipping the saucepan to one side and ladling the brew continuously to dissolve the powdered milk. We drank sickly sweet, room-temperature Frooti drinks while we waited and Pradeep and Dipak chatted with the woman, catching up on news I assumed. I wished I understood what they were talking about.

Jars and plastic containers lined the shelves. A rice-cooker and a food processor sat on a cabinet in one corner. One powerpoint clung to the beam in the middle of the room and a light-switch on another side of the beam had a loose wire running from it up to the fluorescent light above.

As we waited for our tea, I pulled out my phone, found a photo of Tom and showed Abhinav.

"This is my son Tom," I said. "He's seventeen the same as you."

Abhinav took the phone, laughed, and showed it to the others before handing it back. Was he laughing at Tom? His blonde hair? Something else? I smiled and put the phone away and wished Tom was there with us.

Through the kitchen door I could see a walled yard where a young girl and a man squatted breaking rocks with primitive home-made stone hammers. In a corner of the yard cow dung lay spread out drying in the sun. Pink flowers grew along the top of one wall and beyond this more apple trees laden with fruit. The craggy brown mountains rising behind were still blanketed with thick white clouds despite bright sunshine everywhere else. Prayer flags fluttered from every rooftop, some on poles, some strung from pole to pole, and to the south the snowy peaks were covered in fluffy white clouds.

We were now heading into more remote country, climbing higher than I'd ever been, and further from "civilisation", whatever that meant, than I'd ever been. At Samar, Michel Peissel found himself surrounded by Khampa guerillas.

The Khampas, from Kham in eastern Tibet (although guerrilla fighters joined them from other parts of Tibet), became desperate for supplies as the resistance went on. They were trained and supported by the US government, but that support was inconsistent. They had arrived in Mustang from Tibet with little food and ancient munitions. Sporadic drops of munitions, food and medicine were made by the US but they were insufficient. The Khampas were reduced to demanding supplies from the people of Mustang and took to looting and selling priceless artefacts from the monasteries to fund their campaign. So it makes sense that a Western traveller would have been fair game. Peissel managed to placate the Khampas by providing medicines.

After our morning tea break in Samar we continued on, out through another walled gateway over which was built a room. I wondered if it had once served as a guard tower. A trio of chortens stood at the beginning of the path that went steeply down and across a small stream before climbing up and along another narrow precipitous path clinging to the hillside. The steepness of these paths meant I had to walk and so the horses trotted on ahead. As we began to climb again another horse, carrying a wide load of green grass, came towards us followed by its owner. The brown horse needed a wide space to get through with the large packs strapped to its sides, so as the other horse came towards them it caused a traffic jam confusing them all. The foreign horse bolted turning my white horse before it and both took off down and across the stream heading back to Samar. Abhinav took off after it yelling and throwing stones and managed to get ahead of it before it went too far. The owner of the foreign horse simply continued on walking as though nothing happened.

We stopped for lunch at a tiny place called Bhena. It was hardly a village seeming to consist of just the three-roomed tea-house and an outdoor toilet and shower hut. There was a teenage girl holding a small, plump baby, and a girl of about five standing outside when we arrived. After we had unloaded and went inside I pointed at the baby indicating that I wanted to hold it. The girl duly handed it over. I held the baby so I could look at it and it began talking in the way that six-week-old babies the world over talk, with a lot of "oohing" and some excited squeals. I handed him back to his big sister when our tea arrived. Pradeep, Dipak and Abhinav had joined some other men in the kitchen.

Meanwhile the five-year-old had been watching us and began inching closer. I searched for something to show her. I pulled out my phone and took a photo and showed it to her, then showed her how to take a picture of Nev. He suggested she take a "selfie" so I switched the phone around and she was able to take a picture of herself, with which she was delighted. She then took a photo of both of us, but soon this game was exhausted. Having nothing else to show her on the phone without internet, I instead pulled out my pencils and small notebook. I handed her a pencil, opened the notebook and indicated to her to draw something. I expected some babyish scribble, but was surprised when she began to write letters: ABDEF over and over, leaving out the C every time. So I wrote the next few letters and she copied those for a page and so on. I indicated to her that she could keep the pencil and, very pleased with this, went around showing it to each member of the family. If my experience working in Kathmandu where I had to supply all materials was anything to go by, she was unlikely to have anything as luxurious as paper to draw on.

The three rooms of the tea-house were just the room we entered and sat for lunch with the kitchen on one side and a bedroom on the other, in which mattresses covered the floor. Steps outside led to a loft above the bedroom where there were piles of thick colourful blankets. The baby was put to bed while we were there and strung above it was a blow-up plastic ball on a string, the only thing resembling a toy I ever saw in Mustang. When I peeped into the dark room just before we left, the baby was softly mewling and his mother, having finished cooking everyone's lunch, shuffled her shoes off at the door and went in to pick him up.

CHAPTER 10

Lha Gyal Lo

We climbed the pass above Bhena at 3800 metres. To the south were the mountains and thick clouds rising in the river gorge. To the north, our first sight of the yellow, pink and grey undulating hills of the Tibetan plateau. This, at last, was our first sight of the Kingdom of Lo. As they reached the top of the pass, both Dipak and Pradeep called out "Lha gyal lo", meaning "victory to the gods", a traditional greeting upon crossing high passes to appease the deities. We descended eventually reaching the small village of Shyanmochen. The horses stopped themselves outside a tea house, but to their obvious disappointment were made to press on without a break. Our destination was Ghiling which looked close from above, but took many turns and a steep descent on foot before we finally arrived mid-afternoon. It was as though we'd emerged from the stark desert onto a golf course or large bowling green. Ghiling was so impossibly green in that barren landscape that it looked like it was covered in Astroturf.

Cows and horses grazed on softly undulating green pasture fed by small rivulets channelled from the stream that flowed nearby. The leaves of the poplar trees fluttered in the soft breeze. We were well away from the harsh wind of the river gorge now. Stone fences rose and fell with the landscape, walling off yards and fields and some groves of trees to stop the animals grazing on them. These trees are grown for building and when you lay in bed you could look up at a ceiling criss-crossed by their slender trunks if it wasn't otherwise covered by a nursery-themed piece of fabric.

But if I thought I'd arrived at some kind of Lothlorien, where time stood still and the evils of the world could never penetrate, I was delivered a dose of reality when, after I returned home, I spoke to American anthropologist, Sienna Craig. Sienna has written extensively about Mustang. She told me that Ghiling was one of the villages hardest hit by the earthquake. More than sixty houses were destroyed, but no one ever mentioned this to us when we were there. The only evidence we saw was a large crack in the chorten near the monastery. I did a search of "earthquake damage in Ghiling" and found pictures of damaged houses, people living in tents, and piles of rubble. I looked back at my photos and now noticed what I hadn't before: stone walls inside which houses would have stood, houses missing their upper floors, a bulldozer shifting rubble. We'd arrived five months after the earthquake so most of the damage had been cleared away, but I wondered where all those people from the sixty-odd houses lost had gone.

As we approached one of the lodges a man and woman looked up and called out something. They didn't look happy. A loud discussion ensued. Neville and I sat on a wooden seat by the fence, he exhausted from a hard day of climbing, and waited. I'd resigned myself to camping that night when Dipak came over and said, "Please come," and we were led through a small gate into a walled yard and into the guest house. On either side of the doorway was a garden edged with upended Tuborg beer bottles. We entered a short passageway that led into an interior courtyard bathed in green light from the green plastic covering that formed the roof. A sign on the opposite wall showed a faded photo of Ghiling with New Kumla Hotel & Restaurant, Ghiling-3, Mustang written across it. We climbed a steep rickety stairway to the balcony above and were shown to our rooms. Here we had electric light (when the power was on) but no powerpoint to charge our phones. We shared a squat toilet but did have the luxury of a hot gas-powered shower. Dipak brought our packs up and we unpacked for the night.

As the light faded, Neville went out for his usual reconnoitre while I, tired and feeling the altitude again, sat at the window of our room and stared out at this beautiful, tragic village as though it might disappear if I looked away, so green and unreal was it. Our horses had been penned in a yard just below and I watched them scratching each other's manes. In the yard next to them a small corner had been sectioned off with roughly cut pieces of wood, and two fluffy brown calves lay sleeping in the hay. On the barren yellow-grey slope watching over Ghiling were two red monasteries and a large striped chorten. Apart from the earthquake damage it seemed like not much had changed since 1964.

At about five, there was a soft knock on the door and Dipak appeared announcing "dinnnerrr orrrrderrr" and holding a menu with pad and pen. Day three of the carb-fest which constitutes the trekking menu on every trail in Nepal and we were still able to find things we felt like eating, but as the days wore on, choosing between potato, noodles, rice, pizza, and pasta with the same basic flavourings of tomato and cheese, or the different soups which were really the same soup with different things added, for dinner and lunch, became wearying if not down-right depressing. One night I hopefully ordered chicken soup, thinking this would be good when I was feeling ill from the altitude. I'd already tried the garlic soup, which was garlic added to a powdered soup base.

"I don't think this is really chicken," said Pradeep.

He was right. It was just garlic soup without the garlic. The only fresh thing we ate were the ubiquitous apples.

As we sat with Pradeep each night before dinner, I picked his brain about Mustang.

"Pradeep, do they still do sky burials here?" I asked him as we sat in the dining room that night. A lack of wood for cremation, hard ground and the dry landscape mean that sky burials have traditionally been performed in Mustang and Tibet out of necessity. These involve cutting the body into pieces and setting them out to be eaten by vultures.

"Ahhh," he began, "They used to do the sky burial, but now, I'm-a not so sure. You should watch a film called "Himalayan Caravan".

He told me in the past he had taken trekkers to see where sky burials took place, but only from a distance and never to actually watch one.

"They look and see where is many vultures and then do ceremony there. I don't like actually to see this happen," he said, making a face.

"It would be terrible to have the job of cutting up the body," I said. He nodded in agreement and made another face.

"You watch the movie. One time when I take trek in Dolpo I go to the house of the man who is in this movie," he added proudly.

I did eventually watch this movie and a documentary about the tradition of sky burial. The man tasked with butchering the bodies admitted to drinking raksi before undertaking the task, particularly if it was someone he knew. After dismembering the corpse, the bones are ground up and sometimes mixed with yak butter. These are fed to the vultures first. The entire body must be consumed by the birds or demons will take the deceased person's spirit.

I find it almost impossible to imagine the body of someone I know, especially someone I love, being treated in this way; it is reducing the body to its most basic state: meat. But really, the only difference between sky burial and allowing a body to rot in the ground, or to be cremated is visibility. And like most things that are usually unseen, they are fascinating to some people. In Tibet, Chinese tour companies will take tourists to watch sky burials, for a fee. They either forget or don't care that this is a person's funeral, someone whom others loved.

On our journey through Tibet, not long after setting out from Lhasa, we stopped for a break by the river and I remarked to our guide, Tenzin, how inviting the water looked for a swim. As we set off again he pointed to where there were a lot of prayer flags strung up and told us this was where water burials were performed. He said in areas where there are not enough vultures this is an alternative. Suddenly a swim in the river didn't seem so attractive and I pictured myself breast-stroking along and the odd head or limb floating past, trailing crimson in its wake.

I asked Tenzin if babies were given sky burials.

"No," he replied. "When a baby dies it is put into a clay pot and buried. Then we say prayers so that it has a better life next time."

The other Rose's skull was fractured before she had even had a chance to be born, fractured by an incompetent doctor, or an impatient doctor exerting too much force on a pair of forceps. What that experience can have been like for my mother, I can't stand to imagine. Rose lived for twenty-four hours.

I only know about David's death from the fragments told to me by my sisters, told in whispers , told like it was a dirty secret. This is how I imagine the events of that cold July night in 1965.

Their little brother was ten months old when he was bathed that night, dressed in warm pyjamas and sat in his highchair in the kitchen. While my mother cooked dinner, one of my sisters sat and fed him mashed meat and vegetables, scraping the excess as it oozed down his chin and spooning it back into him. He chuckled and banged on the plastic table of the highchair, then he whinged and shook his head when he didn't want any more. Then he was cleaned up, given a bottle, and put to bed in the cot in the room he shared with two sisters.

Winters in that house were cold. The only heating was in the lounge room, where we would run from the bathroom to get dressed in our pyjamas warming by the heater. Our beds were warmed with electric blankets, but in the mornings it was icy cold. It was my father's habit to peer at the thermometer in the hallway when he got up to make everyone tea and toast. "It's one degree," he would announce as he handed us our mugs. "There's a frost!"

After the baby was put to bed, one of my sisters went into the room she shared with him. She crept over to look at her baby brother sleeping and immediately called out to Mum. He wasn't breathing. Mum came running in and started screaming, which caused Dad to come running. He scooped his son up and ran into his and Mum's room. My sisters watched from the hallway while Dad performed CPR and Mum ran past them, out the front door and down to the doctor on the corner. There was a frantic phone call to the nuns up at the convent to, "Please pray for my little boy," then the ambulance arrived, the officers ran in, and everyone rushed past my sisters and out the door again with my mother calling out, "Kneel down and say the rosary," before the screen door slammed and my sisters were left standing in the hall as the warmth drained out and the cold night air crept in. Then they knelt down by their beds and said the rosary.

He was buried next to Rose, which is why my parents were forced to tell my other siblings about her, then all mention of him was forbidden. My brother and eldest sister, away at boarding school in Sydney, were given the news by their respective superiors. The youngest sister, only five-years-old, was sent to stay with friends. Dad and my other two sisters went to the funeral. I guess my mother took to her bed. The day after he died, Mum packed up all of her baby son's things. The following evenings were spent drinking with a friend. I don't know where my father went, maybe the pub or the RSL.

Sixteen months later, I was born. When I was old enough to notice that the baby in the photo on Mum's dressing table, and the baby in the photo hanging in the hall with all the other baby portraits wasn't living with us, my mother told me that was the little boy who died of suffocation when he was ten months old. She didn't get emotional about it, she just did what she always did: she kept moving.

In Lo Manthang, I would discover they had another way of dealing with children who died.

At dinner that night, we were joined by the three Russians who had flown up to Jomsom with us, the very big man and two women, only one of whom had enough English to carry on a conversation. We would meet these three on and off during the trek. They had brought their own Russian salami with them and the big man, very jolly after several Lhasa beers, a wide grin spread across his red face, offered us some. We had already eaten by that time and as much as I appreciated the offer, salami after dal bhat and apple fritters was more than I could stomach, particularly as I was feeling ill from the altitude.

Next morning, after breakfast, Pradeep took us up to the monastery overlooking Ghiling. The night before he told us he was hoping to take us but wasn't sure who had the key and since the monks would be out performing a ceremony in one of the houses he didn't know if he'd be able to get it. But he did, and we walked through the laneways between the stone walls, accompanied by Dipak and climbed up the slope, past the large chorten, cracked from the earthquake, to the bigger of the two red monasteries. In the smaller one further up, Pradeep told us, women were forbidden, but it was locked anyway and he didn't have that key.

As in most of the monasteries in Mustang, photos were not allowed for fear that, knowing what is inside, people may return and steal the valuable statues, paintings and other objects. It was a valid fear, because back in 1992, when Mustang was first opened to tourists, thangkas and statues were stolen from the Ghiling monastery. Since then someone always slept on a bed in the entry room to guard the place.

A large photo of Sakya Trizin, head lama of the Sakya sect of Buddhism, dominated the room, dimly lit by a square skylight. Plump and womanly, he looked like a cuddly grandmother. One monk was present and Pradeep paid him our entrance fee plus extra for a butter lamp which he then invited me to light. Brought up as a Catholic, I was strangely moved by this gesture and marvelled at the similar feeling of reverence I felt standing in that quiet space amongst all those sacred objects, lighting this butter lamp just as I had lit candles in churches at home. The monk then dipped a brush into a plastic container of water and shook it over mine and the other lamps and then over us, all the while intoning prayers.

"This is for safe journey," said Pradeep, with his customary giggle.

This done, the monk then went about his own prayers, ringing a bell and banging a large hanging drum while Pradeep showed us around. The 108 books of Buddhist scripture were tucked into square compartments on one side of the statues, which were set behind glass. The walls were covered in thangkas.

Thanking the monk, we stepped outside and climbed onto the roof, from where we could see the whole village.

"You see that house over there," said Pradeep, pointing northwest to a small house sitting by itself on open flat ground beyond the village, "that is the way we will be going today." A narrow track could just be seen snaking its way out of the valley towards the cloud-wreathed hills, and the Nyi La pass, the highest point in Mustang.

CHAPTER 11

Apple Pie at the Royal Hotel

The Nyi La is at 4100 metres and the poor horses felt every one of those metres as did Neville. We zigzagged our way up the rough trail, the horses stopping at every bend panting heavily, their eyes popping with the effort. I leant forward until I was lying along the horse's back and rubbed the side of its neck, feeling sorry for it. I didn't know whether this made the horse feel better, but thought it might be some antidote to the yelling and stone throwing that it endured from Abhinav and Dipak. "Ch, ch," was their gentle sound of encouragement. When they became really frustrated with the slow pace they'd yell something that sounded like "Shallang!"

"This horse lazy," Dipak remarked to me one day.

I doubted a horse could actually be lazy. Having to carry fifty kilos of human up a steep rise would make me feel pretty lazy.

Abhinav and I reached the top first so stopped for a rest and a drink while we waited for the others. They arrived one by one, and sat down with relief to catch their breath. To the west dark heavy clouds still hung so low over the hills they almost obscured them completely. That way looked forbidding and indeed a couple of vultures could be seen circling high up, their black bodies and wings stark against the grey-white cloud.

"Maybe is something dead up there, I think so," said Pradeep.

I thought again of the sky burials.

The Annapurna range was still visible to the south, also obscured but by white fluffy cloud; to the north the endless undulating hills of the Tibetan plateau. In the valley below was the village of Ghemi. Terraces of green and orange fell away from the village towards the river gorge. On the other side were the faded terraces of an abandoned village. Pradeep said it had moved because of lack of water. Groves of poplar trees stood to one side of the small collection of white square buildings and a milky blue stream could just be glimpsed flowing in the gorge below it.

We stopped for lunch in Ghemi at the Royal Hotel, so named because it was owned by the King of Mustang's sister. We entered the interior courtyard and saw a boy sitting on the ground next to a huge pile of small green and red apples, cutting them into pieces which were forming another pile on his other side. Beside this sat a copper basin filled with water floating on which were plastic water lily flowers. Arranged around the balcony above were pots of geraniums, making the whole area, lit by the skylight, like a cool green oasis after seeing nothing but barren hills for hours. There was a panoramic picture of Lhasa just under the window above. We were ushered upstairs and into the dining room and when we accepted the offer of fresh apple juice the woman expressed her relief.

"I have so many apples, I don't know what to do with them," she said laughing. "I give the less perfect apples to my cows and dry some for use during winter, but with the others I make apple pie. Will you have some of my apple pie?" she asked hopefully.

We nodded. I really didn't want apple pie, but she looked so hopeful I couldn't say no. Given Nepali versions of pizza were nothing like what we would call pizza I didn't feel optimistic about the pie.

There was a photo of the King and Queen of Mustang on a small table in the corner, as well as a photo of an unknown monk. Both pictures were draped with silk katas. Above these, on the wall, were pictures of various buddha statues, also draped in katas. I was looking at these when the woman brought our juice in. She put the drinks down and came over to me. She knelt up on the bench seat and pointed out the window.

"See the pass up there?" she said. I knelt next to her and looked. "When I see people coming from the pass there, I straight away start making dal bhat. Then as soon as they arrive it is ready and they don't have to wait."

She seemed very pleased with herself for this bit of foresight, but I wondered what happened if the person didn't stop, or they went to a different house, or they didn't want dal bhat for lunch. I didn't want dal bhat for lunch. But I felt a strange feeling of camaraderie or sisterhood kneeling with this woman from a totally different place and culture looking out the window. I think it must have a been a symptom of being in the company of men all day, every day; I was missing female company. But I am also strangely reassured when I share something as simple as this with someone from another part of the world.

On my first visit to Nepal I sat one morning with our host mother at the kitchen table topping and tailing beans, just as I did at home, just as I had seen my own mother do when I was growing up. It gave me a vague sense of reassurance. I had to prepare dinner every night just as women in Nepal had to prepare dinner every night. We were all in the same boat. Even on an epic journey someone has to do the cooking.

Our host pointed at a building being constructed across the narrow street.

"We are building a new lodge," she said. I thought this very optimistic since tourist numbers were so low after the earthquake and so many lodges and shops had closed.

"Do you want to see my monastery?" she asked me. "I also have a little shop."

"Yes, ok," I said.

"Just going to look at the shop," I said to Neville.

"Thanks I'll stay here," he replied.

It was like a small version of a monastery. It was a dimly lit room and the walls were covered with paintings of buddhas. Butter lamps and small bowls of water were lined up along a shelf at one end. In a small glass cabinet above these were three gold statues wreathed in orange katas. To the left were the usual 108 sacred books. There were brass or copper vases and teapots along the shelf, some with large arrangements of plastic flowers. Two long tables, one against the wall under the buddhas, one in the middle of the room, groaned with metal artefacts, some encrusted with turquoise and other semi-precious stones. There were small conch shells, short daggers, small metal bowls, statues, and dorjes or vajras, those double-ended things, like a whisk with two ends, that are used in Buddhist ceremonies, meant to represent a lightning bolt. But it all looked like the same stuff sold in innumerable shops in Thamel in Kathmandu, and I suspect came from the same place that mass-produces them.

The table in the middle of the room had more jewellery, things I could at least wear and give as presents.

"I make this jewellery with my sister and our friends during the winter," she told me.

She picked up a string of yak-bone beads, each bead intricately carved with *Om mane padme hum* in Tibetan script. They at least didn't look like the tacky mass-produced things. So I bought these and a silver bangle, because I quite liked them, but also because I felt I should buy something. She charged me twenty US dollars for each item, which I suspected was probably a rip off, but since they were nice souvenirs and it wasn't as though Mustang was bristling with shops, I didn't mind. By the time I got home, the silver was wearing off the bangle, revealing the copper underneath. I gave the beads to a friend.

After our main course we were served the much-promoted apple pie, a huge triangle of apple and gluey pastry layers. I ate as much as I could to be polite and carefully wrapped the rest in a paper napkin for later, knowing full well I'd never eat it.

On the way out of Ghemi, we passed a crumbling fort, a former palace, then, following Pradeep up several steps, we crossed a small wooden bridge under which bubbled a fast-flowing milky blue stream. Strings of tattered prayer flags were tied to a pole at each end and across the bridge, and fluttered in the afternoon breeze. We followed a narrow path along the stream towards our next stop, the village of Tragmar.

CHAPTER 12

Tragmar

Tragmar sits underneath towering red cliffs dotted in parts with high caves. The name Tragmar means "red cliffs". The red of the cliffs are said to be from the blood of a demoness who had come to live in Mustang. Padmasambhava (also known as Guru Rinpoche), the Buddhist master who brought Buddhism from India to Tibet in the eighth century, chased the demoness and struck her with his dorje, tearing her open. Her blood was emptied onto the cliffs of Tragmar. Her intestines are under a long mane wall nearby, and her heart, cut into 108 pieces, lies under chortens where the monastery of Lo Ghekar was built.

After tea and biscuits at the the Tenzin Hotel and Guest House, Neville and I wandered along by the stream and past stubbled fields towards the cliffs. High up were caves, one with a broken fluted piece of stone, orange and grey striped, pressed into the opening. Below was a small crumbling chorten with bare sticks poked into the top and tied to which were ragged prayer flags. The cliff wall behind and the stone base underneath were painted with red, grey and white stripes. The red and dark grey cliffs loomed above like statues of the Gods, possessed of a forbidding power. Above and behind these rose cliffs of butter yellow. We walked into an area surrounded on three sides by the red cliffs and I could see a narrow gap on the left that insidiously tempted me in, but there was something sinister about it; I could almost hear Pradeep warning against going in there, imagining I'd be lost forever. I felt better walking away and back to the green groves of trees and the green and pink, post-harvest stubbled fields, soft in the light of late-afternoon. We wandered along stone walls and across crude wooden bridges. In a partially harvested field by a small red monastery, sat a group of young people in a circle, the boys in baseball caps, the girls in head scarves. They seemed to be just sitting and chatting and I wondered what young people did in this isolated place.

We passed one white adobe house with blue-painted door and window frames, the stone around them painted black. Stairs led to the front door, and underneath two wooden doors led to a storage area and a place for the animals. Outside a toddler with a grubby face and grubby clothes played with a long piece of wood and a twisted piece of tin, regarding us with suspicion as we walked by. Hay lay drying in the yard next to him and was piled up against the wall of the house and on the tops of the stone fences.

As the light began to fade, we made our way back, crunching our way on fallen leaves though the narrow laneways formed by the stone fences and groves of poplar trees. In front of us the valley opened to reveal the snow-capped mountains to the south, wreathed as ever in cloud, distant, but never leaving us. We passed a rough dirt soccer pitch and volleyball court next to a school. As we came up to the lodge, Abhinav was sitting on the ledge outside holding a packet of cigarettes. I jokingly scolded him and, with a guilty look, to my surprise he put them back in his pocket. When we first arrived that afternoon and walked up the passage into the courtyard, he spotted a mirror and immediately went over to check himself out, running his fingers though the mop of orange-dyed hair before giving himself a satisfied smirk.

Here we had hot water from a solar heater on the roof, but no actual shower. By mixing the scalding water from the tap in the rough bathroom with cold water from the tap in the toilet you could have yourself a warm bucket wash. Hot water always cost extra and Pradeep took this cost out of the money we had paid him.

"We don't need hot water do we?" Neville asked me.

"No. Makes no difference if there's no actual shower," I replied.

So Neville told Pradeep we could do without hot water to save him money.

"No, I don't think this is very good idea," he replied. "Is better you wash with warm water. If you wash with cold water, maybe you get a cold."

That night at dinner were a French couple, but like nearly all of the French people we met (and there were a lot) they had no interest in talking to us. We never saw the Germans again and the Russians must have taken a different route but they eventually reappeared.

Pradeep sat with us as usual while we ate our dinner, rugged up in down jacket and beanie now as the evenings grew colder and clutching a glass of hot lemon and rum. On a table in the corner were a few things for sale—the usual bits of jewellery, dorjes, statues—but there were also the two souvenirs I had decided I wanted: a piece of striped woollen Tibetan fabric that all the women wore, and a saligram. Saligrams, or Ammonite fossils, are smooth black stones that, when cut open, reveal a perfect spiral something like a snail shell. They are relics from before the Himalayas formed and the area was covered by the Tethys Ocean.

About fifty million years ago the Indian and Eurasian tectonic plates collided to push these mighty mountains up and out of the ocean, leaving behind these beautiful fossils. The Hindus believe they are the Earthly incarnation of the goddess Vishnu. Ever since I watched Brian Cox search in vain in the river bed for one of these fossils on his "Wonders of the Universe" program I was determined to get one if I ever went there. He searched in vain because the Kali Gandaki river bed is regularly scoured for them. At Kagbeni we saw men walking along the river bed, eyes to the ground, searching, and with good reason: they are easy money. Many places along our route sold saligrams, you can buy them from shops and stalls in Thamel and I even found an online store based in Cornwall flogging them for as much as five hundred pounds.

That afternoon I'd lifted the sheet covering the items for sale and examined what was on offer. I found a perfect saligram, smooth, cold, and black, scalloped around one edge, split in half to reveal a beautiful, clear spiral, and a striped, slightly grubby, Tibetan apron and decided to make them mine. So at dinner I told Pradeep I wanted to buy these things and asked him to speak to the lodge owner.

"Mmm..maybe tomorrow when you've had a better look," he replied without making eye-contact.

"But I've had a look and I know what I want to buy," I said.

"Mmm..maybe better to look tomorrow when the light is better," he replied without looking at me.

I looked at Neville. He shrugged his shoulders and in both our minds went that oft-repeated conversation we had every time we travelled in Nepal. Why did they do this? Why did they do that? So many things appeared to us like the total opposite of logic. Plus there were issues of caste and rules of protocol we couldn't begin to understand.

Did Pradeep think I shouldn't give them the business, waste my money, make the horses carry two more things? The conversation was clearly at an end, but I was annoyed by his refusal to explain what the problem was. But the Nepalese will never say "no"; they'll just dodge the issue. I could have asked the owner myself, but since Dipak was the one who delivered our meals, we never saw them and I didn't feel comfortable poking about looking for them, quite apart from the fact I couldn't speak Nepali. I could see the two things I wanted but now didn't know how I could get them. I could either suck it up for now or make a scene. It would never do to make a scene because losing your temper is not done or you will lose all respect. I still had many days left to spend with Pradeep; I had to accept that he was in charge.

I woke early next morning and, still tucked in the warmth of bed, sat looking out the window at the village starting its day in the cool morning air. For a change, Neville still lay snoring beside me. I usually woke to find he had gone off exploring. There was a hose by the stream on the side of the road just outside the lodge. A woman in traditional dress wearing a "Free Tibet" beanie squatted by the hose cleaning her teeth, her pinafore tucked up out of the way, revealing leggings underneath. I heard the tinkling of horse bells and three people came galloping along, two men and one woman with a baby strapped to her back; they pulled up briefly to greet the woman at the hose, then spurring their horses, galloped towards the cliffs. Bare-backed horses stopped to drink from the puddle of water made by the hose, which ran continuously, the water flowing down the bank into the stream. Their owner strolled slowly behind them, hands clasped behind his back. A man came out and squatted by the hose cleaning something while a little girl in a red dress and leggings leaned over watching closely. The cliffs to the north west were once again shrouded in heavy dark grey clouds.

After breakfast, as we were making our way along the passage to go outside, Pradeep hurried in, beanie on, hands jammed into his jacket pockets.

"You want to see blue ship? There are blue ship over near cliffs," he said excitedly.

We followed him out into the crisp air and over towards the red cliffs. There, making their way up the sloping ground at the base of the cliffs were three blue sheep. Himalayan blue sheep, or bharals are found throughout the Himalayas, but their grey-blue colouring makes them extremely hard to spot. I photographed the sheep but when I looked at the photos they weren't there. Only in the video footage I took can be seen three of the palest shadows moving across the ground, but as soon as they stop moving they are invisible.

A small shop had opened on the ground floor of the lodge. There was a young girl standing outside the shop holding a chubby baby, rugged up in a quilted pink jacket and pants and a blue and white beanie. A bracelet of cloth and string was tied around one fat wrist. I smiled and pointed at the baby and she handed it over. Neville accused me of doing the baby tour of Upper Mustang, and while I'm not overly fond of babies, holding the odd one is quite nice.

Then Pradeep, called out to me.

"Rose, you can go now and buy those things if you want."

I'd almost forgotten about them, thinking I'd just have to get them elsewhere. I still had no idea what the problem was the night before, but Pradeep mentioned later that officials used to search for and confiscate saligrams at Jomsom airport presumably because they are considered sacred. Was there someone in the dining room that evening who Pradeep was worried might disapprove of the buying and selling of saligrams? The owners of the lodge obviously weren't too worried; money surely doesn't get any easier than selling rocks to tourists.

I went up the steep stairs to the dining room followed by a young boy, and picked out the apron and the stone. I asked him how much and he indicated that I should follow him downstairs. While I waited in the inner courtyard he went into a room where I could hear the baby crying. After a short discussion he came out.

"3000 rupees," he said.

I thought this a bit stiff but since there weren't many things I was planning to buy on the trip, it was only about forty dollars, not much money for me but a lot for them, I agreed and handed over the notes. I had my treasures at last.

I've often reflected on why Pradeep was being so difficult the night I asked about buying these things. I wonder if the other people in the room were the problem. I don't remember if I mentioned exactly which things I wanted—the apron and the saligram. Sometimes when I hold the saligram in my hand, I wonder whether I should have taken it. Indigenous Australians believe all things, including rocks, should be left where they belong because they are inhabited by the spirits of that place. No ill has befallen me for removing the stone and it was the inhabitants who sold it to me, and yet I wonder what right I have to possess something considered sacred by a faith that is not my own. And yet, I love the thing, its smooth, cool, black surface and, inside, the intricate spiral formed by a creature that lived millions of years ago. Its beauty and mystery are seductive.

The pack horse all loaded and ready, I mounted my unnamed white mare and we set off. We headed towards the cliffs and turning slightly left at the end of the village, began to climb on a narrow, worn gravel trail, up and out of the valley. We were soon climbing steeply, and already, this early in the day, the horses were pausing after a few steps, breathing hard. Abhinav, in a new pink jacket he'd acquired from somewhere in Tragmar, held onto the tail of the brown horse urging it on with his "ch, ch,". We reached the top through a gap in the cliffs, flanked by huge grey boulders. Prayer flags were tied from one to the pole at the top, surrounded by a cairn, the rocks thrown there for good luck by travellers. We arrived first and Abhinav helped me dismount (although I didn't need help) and the horses wandered off to graze on the sparse grass while we waited. Before us a worn trail snaked away across a plain of gently undulating hills beyond which the vast Tibetan plateau stretched interminably. The wind was already up, whipping the prayer flags. I took out my phone and checked the altimeter: 4050 metres. I looked to the south and saw the Annapurnas, their clear, snow-capped peaks now free of cloud and shining brilliantly in the morning sun.

Dipak appeared, dropped his pack, and skipped back down to where Neville was toiling up the slope. He took Neville's pack and came almost skipping back up again, while Neville, one pole and one foot at a time, made his way up. Pradeep arrived soon after Neville and took a short break to recover. While we were sitting, a man on a horse came galloping up the same steep slope. He paused to exchange a few words with Pradeep and Dipak then galloped away. I watched how easily he managed the horse and felt my own paltry lack of skill. I remounted and we set off again, following slowly in the same direction.

That night I would sleep in Lo Manthang.

CHAPTER 13

Lo Gekar

There were no villages now between Tragmar and Lo Manthang, but at about mid-morning, we approached a small collection of buildings surrounded by several simple red chortens, like small red step-pyramids, dotted by some unseen artist like the final touches around the red and white icing sugar buildings in the middle. This was Lo Ghekar, where the 108 pieces of the demoness' heart were buried. Also called Gar Gompa, or house monastery, Lo Ghekar, meaning "pure virtue of Lo", is the oldest monastery in Upper Mustang. Some men on horses arrived just ahead of us and, after tethering their horses (ours were let free to graze on a stretch of green lawn) approached the monastery where they filed past the prayer wheels, setting them spinning while quietly chanting. The wheels made a rhythmic clanking to accompany the low murmurings of the men's prayers. Pradeep took us into a small room to the left of the main entrance and with him we turned a great colourfully painted prayer wheel three times, turning clockwise in keeping with Buddhist practice. Then we sat on the rough stone steps, grass growing from the cracks, and waited while Pradeep found the person who would allow us in. It was warm in the sun and we both enjoyed the rest after a couple of steep climbs already that morning. A few large trees grew near the monastery and above us a strange bird repeated a harsh note.

"What is that bird?" I asked Abhinav, who was sitting a little removed from us, looking tired and bored.

"Cark," he replied. "Cark" was certainly the sound the bird was making but I doubted that was its actual name.

Pradeep then reappeared and called us in. We went up the steps and through an entrance over which a worn and stained, thick brown curtain hung, edged in white with pink diamond shapes on the band across the middle. At the top was a short yellow pelmet and the same fabric hung over most of the doors and windows. The two sides of the curtain were tied back leaving a triangular opening. Leaving the bright sunlight outside, we stepped into the gloom. Our guide greeted us with "Namaste" and told us straight up that this monastery was "thirteen hundred old". Shoes off, we ducked through a low door into a room, the walls of which were covered with paintings. It smelled of smoke and incense. On the right, above a cabinet, were small paintings of buddhas in wooden frames. I counted sixty there, but there were more on the other side of the room. Further in, set in an alcove behind glass, were life-sized statues of two goddesses, one seated on a cow, the other on a horse; the latter, our guide told us, was a protector goddess.

In the main monastery room the Buddha sat in the centre of the far wall behind glass illuminated by a light inside. Pradeep, after a rapid conversation with the guide, explained in his faltering English, mixing it with French grammar if not words, that this was a statue of Padmasambhava, who founded the monastery. "When he first time comes from India, and they bring to Tibet, mmm...Tibet also, after India, Nepal, then Tibet, in that time he is meditation this place."

I checked that I understood him. "So, he came up from India and on his way to Tibet to bring Buddhism to them, he stopped here to meditate and that's why a monastery was built here?"

"Eee, yes," he replied at little uncertain. "In my place, I also have the statue in my house—a small one—and in the earthquake time, all is fall down," he added, and giggled.

Using the torch on my phone I wandered around the room looking at the paintings before Pradeep called me over to one corner and we crouched down to where there was a small image of the Buddha, shaped from the rock wall itself, about a foot high. It was smooth as though worn over time and in the creases were remnants of gold paint.

"Tara," the guide said.

"Tara?" I replied.

"Ya, Tara." I had no idea what he meant. I later learnt that Tara (there are twenty-one of them) is a female incarnation of the Buddha. Pradeep searched hard for the words to explain.

"This is, errr, nobody is, err, it's a-come just out like that. Maybe when some, errr, meditation, err, Padmasambhava it comes like that."

I had been concentrating hard to understand him, then realised what he meant.

"So it just appeared?" I said

"Yes!" replied Pradeep.

"So it just appeared in the stone?"

"Ya," replied Pradeep and the guide together, nodding and smiling broadly.

These carvings are known as "self-emanating" statues and are found throughout Mustang and Tibet.

Throughout the tour the low murmurings of the men who had arrived just ahead of us continued in the background. We emerged into the sunlight wearing small yellow katas given as part of the deal and to give us good luck. The strange bird was still making its harsh noise.

"What *is* that bird?" I asked Pradeep.

"Err, is a crow," he replied, but he rhymed it with "now".

I needed the toilet and after following the directions found a free-standing building perched above a steep drop that fell away down to the river. It was a rough squat toilet, just two boards set into the floor with a gap in the middle. I tried to ignore the enormous pile of excrement underneath. I stood up and looked out the small square window. The view to the east looked over the terraced fields of the village of Marang, pink and fading green, edged with dark green trees, like all the other villages, brimming with life as the desert mountains jealously closed in around them. Craggy bare hills stretched away, and to the south, and white peaks guarded the horizon.

When I returned Pradeep asked, "Err, Rose, would you like to have some noodle soup?"

I did not want to insult the monks' offer of hospitality, but the thought of more noodles at morning tea when much the same would be offered at lunch and dinner, made me feel sick.

"Ahhh, nnooo?" I replied with a rising inflection trying to be as polite as possible.

"No?"

"Maybe tea?"

"Tea? Ok," and he turned and led us through another low door into the interior courtyard and up the stairs to a small dining room, its walls painted a violent shade of orange with a painted border at the top resembling bright green curtains. Two bright silk thangkas hung down one wall. Unseen monks made our milky, sickly sweet tea.

Leaving Lo Ghekar, we made our way down and onto a small wooden bridge, its railings crumbling, and across the milky-blue rapids of the stream which ran through the gully below. The gushing waters briefly drowned out the sound of the wind and the tinkle of the horses' bells.

And on across the barren land. With no village at which to stop for lunch, Pradeep had packed a picnic of yak cheese, tinned Chinese sardines, flat disks of Tibetan bread from Tragmar, and apples from Kagbeni. After climbing another pass, we spread ourselves on a patch of rough grass and lounged in the sun eating our lunch. It was just about the best thing we'd eaten since beginning the trek. The sardines were the first thing resembling meat that we'd eaten since Kagbeni. They were salty, covered in a tomato sauce and salty black beans, the Tibetan bread deliciously chewy.

It was hard to believe that we were still on the same planet. Apart from the cairn, there was nothing manmade in sight. The whole world spread out around us, empty. We lay under a piercing sun, merciless at that altitude. My hands were burnt red raw on the first day, despite sunscreen, so I'd had to add my woollen gloves; a great look added to the helmet and hat. Out of the corner of my eye I caught movement and looked to see a small lizard, it's sand-yellow skin with faded green patches merging seamlessly with the ground. Its yellow cat's eyes regarded me with contempt; it seemed to say, "I've been here for millions of years. Who are you to come to this place?"

We heard a distant dog bark and looked up to the top of the hill behind us. Three dogs stood looking out like sentinels.

"Sheep dog," said Dipak.

"Maybe is some sheep grazing near, I think so," said Pradeep.

"Pradeep, have you ever seen a snow leopard," I asked.

"Yes. One time, I taking trek and walking bit away from group, I look up and see snow leopard up on the hill. So I turn and go back to tell them, suddenly I see, there is other one, err, sleeping."

"Quite close to you?"

"Yes, very close, and …" his eyes widened and holding his hands in front he took a deep breath. "Was very big one."

It was downhill for the rest of the day. In some parts the trail became steep and too slippery with loose stones to ride. I got off the horse, happy to walk for a while. My knees ached and then screamed the longer I sat on the horse, and when my feet touched the ground, pain shot through my legs, easing off after a few steps. I couldn't for the life of me understand why anyone would ride a horse for pleasure.

CHAPTER 14

The Walled City

This trip had been at least two years in planning, in my mind at least. The thought that I, a girl from Bellingen, New South Wales and a culture entirely foreign, would actually be setting my feet on the streets of Lo Manthang, breathing the air that whipped around and drifted within its walls, touching those ancient walls, built for protection against threats I could scarcely imagine, that my life would, albeit in a small way, intersect with the people there, so that our histories were momentarily shared, felt as incredible as the thought of one day standing on Mars. The promise of Lo Manthang had buoyed me up and kept me going through the tedium of daily living and the larger hurdles of life. When I walked the dog, I told myself I was in training for the journey. It had been the goal of a new chapter in my life as I left my home town for the last time.

For Michel Peissel, I guess achieving Lo Manthang was more momentous than for me, because the only proof he had that it even existed was from the scant bits of writing by Toni Hagan, David Snellgrove, and Giuseppe Tucci, all of whom visited the city only briefly. The very first mention of Mustang in English literature is by William J. Kirkpatrick, a Colonel with the East India Company who was apparently the first Englishman ever to set foot in Nepal, way back in 1793. He was sent there to mediate between China and Nepal, the former having launched an attack on the latter. The British got involved because they didn't fancy having China on the doorstep of their colony. Even today Nepal serves as a buffer between these two powerful countries and is at the mercy of both.

Of Mustang, Kirkpatrick wrote:

> The part of Him-a-leh directly to the north of Beeni is called Mooktinath (or Sri Mooktinath) within half a mile of which the Gunduck takes the name Saligrami, the consecrated stones so called abounding particularly in that part of its bed. The source of the river is said to be situated Northward of Mookti, in the direction of Mustang, and not far from Kagbeeni. Mustang is a place of some note in upper Tibet, or Bhoot, and twelve journies from Benisheh.

I don't know where Benisheh is, and when I Googled it all I got were posts boasting "Sexy Girls Photos—Sexy Girls Videos". Whatever goes on in Benisheh, it is "twelve journies" from Mustang.

Before we saw Lo Manthang we saw, over to the west, the red monastery of Namgyal, perched on a rocky outcrop, halfway up the mountain. High on the crest of a barren brown hill to the north were the ruins of a round tower and a wall—the fortress of Ketcher Dzong, built by the warrior and first king of Mustang, Ame Pal, who founded the kingdom of Lo around 1380. We saw Lo Manthang long before we actually arrived. It seemed close, but as we wearily trudged towards it, with that feeling of fatigue that begins to descend when you know you're close to your destination, it didn't seem to come any closer. Peissel's photo of Lo Manthang is one of the only colour plates in his book, and shows a compact walled city, surrounded by neat green, walled fields, its palace and monasteries standing clear above the the other buildings inside.

What we saw was a sprawl of buildings and green trees in the midst of which was a concentration of buildings, the red monasteries and white palace still standing tall above the rest. It was hard to see a clear wall. Unlike Peissel, none of whose party had ever seen Lo Manthang, our "staff" had all been to Lo Manthang several times. It was just another stop on the job for them, and a couple of days rest, especially for Abhinav, who was clearly bored with the whole expedition. So, far from it being a momentous arrival, we simply ambled up the street along the outside of the south wall to our lodge, relieved to be finally stopping for more than one night.

I wish I could say I was overcome at having finally attained my goal; that I had finally arrived at the fabled walled city and wax lyrical about my dream becoming reality. But when, sitting in our mundane surroundings, beset by the demands and anxieties of everyday living, we imagine being somewhere we perceive to be more exciting, we forget that we inevitably take those everyday concerns and anxieties with us; what, in fact, we take is ourselves. Gertrude Stein summed it up long before me: "There is no there there". I tried to feel it. When we saw it from a distance I did feel a hint of excitement but the feeling of just wanting to get off the horse drowned it out. I'd had a headache all day from the altitude and the reality was, on reaching the lodge all I wanted to do was have a cup of tea and a lie down.

My effort to get to Lo Manthang was to prove to myself that it really existed, and if so, that it really was that one place in the world frozen in time. All I knew about it was what I'd read in Michel Peissel's book and the scant article on Wikipedia. Which is more than Peissel had. And although my expedition, if it can be called that, was a pale imitation of Peissel's, with his yak caravan, no guide, and no map, I had still achieved something great. I had ridden a horse through a desert for five days to reach a place few people (at least in Australia) have even heard of. A place mysterious and fairly inaccessible. I wasn't expecting to find Shangri-La and I didn't, but for the rest of my life, if I never did anything else, I could say I'd once ridden a horse to Lo Manthang. Ok, through the desert on a horse with no name.

I envy the women explorers—Freya Stark, Gertrude Bell, Dervla Murphy, and our own Kay Cottee, Robyn Davidson, and the young Jessica Watson (to name a handful)—who had the fortitude to undertake true journeys into the unknown. I especially envy the early travellers for the fact that it was still relatively safe to travel compared to now. As recently as the 1970s, Dervla Murphy travelled with her six-year-old daughter through Baltistan in Pakistan. Gertrude Bell wandered about in the middle east in long skirts and a big hat (and I dare say, she looked nothing like Nicole Kidman in the movie after several months in the desert). But Dervla Murphy slept perfectly well in a puddle of water, was immune to cold, and was happy to live on whatever food she came across in the villages, even if that meant a steady diet of apricot kernels. And although there were obvious dangers for a woman traveller in Pakistan, Iran, or Ethiopia back then, a woman travelling alone in these places today would likely never be heard of again.

One of the places I'd love to travel to is Timbuktu; another ancient city in the middle of a vast desert and positioned along an ancient trade route. This obsession came on after reading about it in the dreadfully named but fascinating *Bad-Ass Librarians of Timbuktu*. I went so far as sending myself a postcard from there in case the same magic would work again. Through that I made contact with Phil Paoletta, the American who runs the Postcards from Timbuktu venture, set up to provide income to former tour guides now tourists can't visit. The official Australian government advice regarding travel to Mali has their highest rating: Do Not Travel. The Lonely Planet has a chapter about Mali in their Africa guide, but states that sadly it isn't safe to travel there. And you can't get travel insurance. But pretty sure Gertrude and even Dervla never had travel insurance. Nevertheless, I still toyed with the idea and gave Phil a call. He told me Bamako was relatively safe to travel to then, but no one could get to Timbuktu.

"If you try, the soldiers will turn you around," he told me. "You could try stowing away in a boat and come up the river," he suggested, sounding serious.

There's fearless and then there's stupid.

Still, in making it to Lo Manthang I had achieved something but, like the climbers who scale Everest, I still had to make it back down.

When we had unloaded our packs in our room, Neville announced he was going out for a look.

"Well I'm coming too," I said.

"I thought you were going to have a sleep," he replied.

"Well not if you're going out. You're not seeing Lo Manthang before me."

And really, I could hardly attain Lo Manthang only to lie down for a nap. Neville was of course not too tired, despite climbing high passes and walking for six hours. He was so annoying like that.

Lo Manthang is L-shaped and the entry is in the corner of the L. From our lodge, built against the south wall, we followed the wall and turned left on a wide, cobble-stone path, along the middle of which ran a narrow, concrete water channel. A woman washed clothes at a stone tap. Somewhere a goat bleated. In front of us, by a wall of prayer wheels, a calf nibbled at the bits of straw strewn on the path. On the right was a walled tree-garden. The Rinzin Grocery Shop's doors were closed, as were the doors of the Himalayan Handicrafts House. A doorway, over which was a sign reading Lo Manthang Community Library, opened onto a courtyard. The only sounds were the twittering sparrows and the goat.

The wide entry through the stone wall was hung at the front with a short gold, red, blue, and green curtain, and framed either side with thick carved wooden pillars. In its "ceiling" hung prayer flags and talismans to ward off bad spirits. The entry used to be closed every night against invaders, but it's now left open, the heavy wooden door propped open with a rock. We walked through, turned left, then right, and found ourselves standing in front of a small enclosed porch. Like everything else, it was coated in dust. A wooden palate leant against one stone wall inside the porch, which was flanked on both sides by thick wooden pillars. We tipped our heads back to see three more storeys. Above the porch was an open balcony held up by slightly smaller pillars, the room above was partially closed by carved wooden windows, and the room on the top floor had three casement windows with small square panes of dusty glass. The walls were of white adobe like all the houses in Mustang; it was just a much larger version of the other houses, standing four storeys, but it was the only one without piles of wood edging its roof. Grey streaks ran down the rough white walls, and prayer flags fluttered strung from the poles on each corner. There were cracks in the walls and some of the render had fallen away.

"The king and queen and all their servants had to leave because the palace is not safe," said a voice behind us. We turned to see a man standing next to us also looking up at the damaged walls. We were standing outside the front door of the palace.

The word "palace" conjures visions of opulence that in my western mind at least were far from what I was looking at. But compared to all of the other houses in the other villages, and the houses in Lo Manthang, this one was palatial if only by size. This four-storey building, built of mud and stone like all the other buildings in Mustang, had stood for seven hundred years. When Michel Peissel arrived in Lo Manthang, the royal family were living in their summer palace of the time, north-west of Lo Manthang so while he had more than one audience with the King, he never entered the palace. The Nepalese writer, Manjushree Thapa, did meet the King in his palace in the early '90s and describes it thus:

> A rickety wood staircase led to a dark landing that was decorated with a stuffed Tibetan mastiff…Up another stairway was a verandah lined with prayer wheels and painted with Buddhist landscapes…The toilet in the palace…was like others in Lo, with a hole in the middle of the room, except that the room underneath, where excreta was collected for fertiliser, was a giddy three storeys down instead of the customary one.

The 85-year-old king, Jigme Dorje Palbar Bista was twenty-fifth in a direct line descending from Ame Pal, the first king; his queen, Sidol Palbar Bista, was from a noble Tibetan family and reputed to be a great beauty in her youth. They had moved to their residence in Kathmandu after the earthquake and there was speculation they would be too old to return before the palace was repaired. There was sadness in the man's voice and as I looked up at the dark windows of the empty palace I could feel that something was gone, perhaps forever, that I had just missed it. The fact the Tibetan term for the King of Lo means "presence" was now a sad irony.

Just one year later, the King died in Kathmandu having never returned to Lo Manthang. His adopted son (actually his nephew) did not take his place as King of Lo.

The small square below the palace walls, used for ceremonies and gatherings for centuries was full of rubble. A building opposite had collapsed and was being rebuilt.

"Before there is large thangka there," the same man told us, pointing to a high wall overlooking the square. At its base lay broken baskets, a torn plastic feed bag. A sign had been propped against the wall; it read "Minimum Impact Code" and listed things like "Save Fuel", "Don't Pollute".

Leaving the square, we walked down a narrow street alongside which the water channel ran. Narrower passages led off this one, some ending in dead ends at small wooden doors, some opening out onto wider streets. Some tunnelled under the houses which all joined together in one giant fortress, huddled close and secret within the thick walls, sheltered against the wind and whatever enemies had threatened them over the centuries.

I found Lo Manthang it to be one giant maze and no matter how much we walked around I could never get my bearings. It felt like we kept going in circles and when I thought we'd seen it all, Neville assured me we hadn't. We were accosted by a few people asking to "just look in my shop", which offer we declined, but there was one man who was so nice that we relented and went in. The one thing I'd decided I did want to buy for myself and for my long-suffering riding teacher was a horse bell. These metal bells are a bit like the small singing bowls used in Buddhist meditation, and have a magically clear ring. I found one in the shop carved with *Om Mane Padme Hum* in Tibetan script and decided to buy it from the overjoyed owner. I marvelled at the old saddles, pieces of wood held together by thin pieces of leather. The owner began his sales pitch, but I explained that I couldn't possibly fit such a thing in my pack and couldn't ask the poor brown horse to carry it on top of our already huge packs. Neville found a long piece of knitted wool, a wide shallow scoop in the middle.

"Is for throwing stones. To catch animals," said the owner.

"Oh a sling-shot?"

"Yes, yes. Sling-shot."

"You buy it?"

"How much," Neville asked.

"Three thousand rupees."

I looked at Neville. "Go on buy it."

"No, it's too much," he replied.

"Please. I need to pay school fees," the man said. "How much you want to give me?"

"No I don't need it."

"Just buy it," I said through gritted teeth, feeling sorry for the man.

"No," said Neville and hung it back up.

Another tourist had entered the shop soon after us.

"Ya know, I've one of these things that I bought in South America," he told us in a Southern American drawl. "The design is exactly the same. It's amazing."

The shop owner looked hopeful for another sale, but the man waved him away.

"I can't carry anything else, and anyway I got hundreds of these types of things," he said and ducked out through the low door and walked off.

Business was slow. The drop in tourist numbers since the earthquake was evident by the number of closed businesses in Lo Manthang. It looked as though people had just shut up shop and left.

There was "real" coffee rumoured to be found in at least one establishment in Lo Manthang and we found it, just a few doors up from our lodge at the Hotel Mystique. One small coffee machine sat on a counter next to a water purifier and took ten minutes to heat the water, which was no problem for us as we weren't going anywhere else. The proprietor, a tall young woman in traditional dress, told us that since the installation of the solar plant, just outside of the city, things were much better for her business as she could now use her machine all day. The seventy kilowatt plant was installed just two weeks before we arrived, fully funded and constructed by the Chinese government. 300 solar panels now stood in three rows outside the city and power poles lined the streets surrounding Lo Manthang. Electricity wires accompanied the fluttering prayer flags, surreptitiously snaking under walk-ways, attached to the ancient mud walls and hitched above the doorways of monasteries built long before electricity was ever discovered. Before this, Lo Manthang had only limited electricity supplied by micro-hydropower plants and some solar panels. Ironically, Lo Manthang had become the only place in Nepal with a 24-hour electricity supply, which for the inhabitants was life-changing, but which sounded within me a tiny alarm: electricity could only mean huge changes.

There were a couple of Americans and a guy from the Dominican Republic who were staying at the Hotel Mystique and we got chatting to them. Their guide was an ex-monk, born and raised in Lo Manthang.

"How do you feel about the new road?" I asked him

"I don't like it," he replied. "I worry it will bring more people here and our culture will be eroded."

Once, Lobas (as the people of Lo are known) were weeks away from the nearest large settlements, like Pokhara, Lhasa or Kathmandu; weeks away from foreign-made goods and food but also from medical assistance. Now, for a price, they could be in Jomsom in eight hours, albeit after a very bumpy ride in a four-wheel-drive; for more money they could get a helicopter straight to Pokhara or Kathmandu, to modern medical care and everything else the modern world offers.

When I returned home to Australia, I asked Sienna Craig about this concern for the erosion of culture.

"It's a superficial line, really," she told me. She said that Mustang was a very resilient and dynamic place, that they cling fiercely to tradition but also embrace what the modern world offers, but there was a lot of local politics and it is a difficult place as a result.

This tension between the preservation of a unique culture and the desire to embrace the conveniences of the modern world and all of the economic benefits are reflected in the ACAP brochure given out to each tourist at the entry to this restricted area—when they haven't run out. The introduction by the King himself says:

> The challenge we face today is to improve our living conditions and at the same time to strengthen and keep alive our culture.

※ ※ ※

We celebrated that night with hot lemon drinks (made, alas, with a powder, real lemons being a fantasy) laced with Nepalese "Kukri" rum. As usual Pradeep joined us in the dining room before dinner, but this night, as we sat hunched in fatigue and relief over our warm drinks, he produced a small bottle and asked would we like to add "some colour". Now that we were at our highest altitude, at 3,800 metres, and not too adversely affected above slight light-headedness and needing to take three breaths for one good one, we could indulge. Going up it is not a good idea and to be honest, I never felt like drinking, already feeling slightly wobbly, but tonight felt like a celebration and would be the first of many protracted pre-dinner drinks. Pradeep had also brought a packet of salty nuts and seeds, and Dipak poured these onto a plate to go with our drinks. Sometimes he would also join us, clutching a glass of hideous raksi, a clear home-brewed alcohol usually distilled from millet or rice. It is drunk warm and to me it tasted like poison.

So we sat in the dining room, the windows of which looked down on the street below, and became warmer both physically and metaphorically towards our indomitable guide. I had my, by now, slightly dog-eared copy of Michel Peissel's book with me as I wanted to check a few things with him. I asked him about something, casually flashing the book in front of him, saying that it was an old book about Mustang.

"Just let me see who wrote that," he said, and I showed it to him. His eyes widened.

"Oh! Michel Peissel! I know him!"

"Really?"

"Yes. I travelled on a bus with him from Kathmandu to Lhasa in… err…1986!"

I couldn't believe it. He said they had travelled together to Lhasa, but there their paths diverged, Pradeep taking a trek to Mount Kailash, whilst Peissel must have been setting out on his journey to the southeast region of Tibet in the region of Tsari along the sacred Brahmaputra river, one of the first Westerner's to do so.

I showed Pradeep some of the pictures in the book.

"Ah! Pemba!" he exclaimed at a photo of a woman with a lined face, combing the greasy or wet hair of the toddler in her lap. The woman was Peissel's landlady in Lo Manthang. Pemba was the Loba aristocrat that Peissel befriended soon after arriving in Lo Manthang and it was through Pemba that he was able to access and learn much about Mustang. The child in the photo was Pemba's eldest daughter, but Pradeep had known her father. It was like he had rediscovered a long-lost friend.

"He has one son in America and another one in France, I think so," he told me.

Pradeep laughed at how black with soot the woman's face and hands were, saying this was from the yak dung fires that they used to cook over, now replaced with gas.

"Well Michel Peissel died in 2011," I casually remarked. Pradeep looked stricken.

"He died?" he exclaimed. I now reluctantly confirmed it, regretting that I had unwittingly delivered what was very sad news for Pradeep. Peissel died of a heart attack at the relatively young age of 74. The fact that he took "over a hundred packs" of cigarettes on his three-month journey into Mustang might provide one clue as to why.

CHAPTER 15

The Buddha Who is to Come

The next morning began with beating drums. I stood on the roof of the lodge and listened to Lo Manthang waking up. There was chanting going on nearby—it sounded like "Lowwww...lowwww"— and then a drum, beating slowly, gradually speeding up to a steady 1-2-3 rhythm, then returning to a slow steady beating, and then more chanting. The brown sparrows flitted amongst the wood piles around the roof edges, twittering constantly. Children called. Water splashed from the public tap. White clouds pushed up from behind the hills to the north and west and shadowed Ketcher Dzong (dzong is Tibetan for "fort") high up on its barren hill. Men and women herded cattle and goats out and women swept the dirt paths with brooms of dried grass.

I walked out early and alone that first morning and as I approached the entry a small dog resembling a corgi, ambled up to me. Ignoring the warnings about never touching dogs in Nepal for fear of rabies, I reached down and gave it a good scratch behind the ears. As soon as I stopped it jumped up and put its front paws on my leg so I gave it another scratch. I then heard a voice say, in very clear English, "This dog is very beautiful," and looked up to see three small children, a girl and two boys. All wore mismatched clothes—tracksuit pants and hoodies, one a double-breasted pink coat over a green jumper fraying at the cuffs—covered in stains and dirt. Their ruddy, Tibetan cheeks were grimy, and the girl clutched a small packet of something like Cheesels.

"He is very beautiful," I replied to the observation.

I sat down on a ledge outside a shop and the three came over, so I pulled out my phone to take photos and we had some great fun taking selfies, then each of them wanted a separate photo. They all struck the same pose: one hand on the hip, the other hand held up in a peace sign, their faces pulled into cheeky grins, or trying to look cool, flashing white pegs of tiny baby teeth. They giggled in delight when I showed them results. As we were doing this, a woman came up to see what we were up to. When she saw the photos I'd taken of the children she pointed at herself and stood at a distance from me so I could photograph her as well. In the picture she stands proudly, smiling with closed lips, eyes down. She wears a red floral blouse under her pinafore (called a *bukkoo*), dark grey with a pale thin stripe, the usual striped piece of woven material around her hips, edged with a blue border and secured with a narrow belt of the same material decorated with a red and blue cross at intervals—a *kiti* and *kaou*. Around her neck is a string of red and turquoise beads, she wears a gold bangle on her wrist, and earrings made from a dark-coloured stone. I showed her her photo and she chuckled in delight then went on her way. Then a younger, plump woman stuck her head out of the doorway behind us and called sternly to the children. I said "Namaste" and she gave a reluctant angry "Namaste" back. The children hurried to her and she ushered them in.

I felt uncomfortable and slightly guilty. While it's possible she was just a harried mother trying to get her three children ready for the day I couldn't help wondering if there was a level of resentment towards the foreigners visiting Lo Manthang. For those with businesses that serve the tourists they are a benefit, until of course they stop coming which was largely the case when I was there. Otherwise, the Nepalese government earns a lot of money from the visitors while the locals see their villages and children photographed and inspected but earn nothing. Glossy photographic books are produced of Lo Manthang and Upper Mustang but as far as I know the local people don't receive any of the proceeds. Wasn't I just another foreigner come to gawk at an ancient culture?

Back at the guest house the large group of Belgians who'd been staying there were piling into a jeep to travel back to Jomsom. They were a family group, come to inspect an orphanage they'd set up on an earlier trip and to do some trekking. Having trekked to Lo Manthang they were taking the easy-*er* way back. Eight hours bumping around in a jeep was faster but I don't think very pleasant, but I was beginning to fear that I may have to give in and do this. I'd finally, inevitably come down with a cold—despite washing in warm water on Pradeep's advice—and if I get a cold it almost always goes to my chest. This could not happen at almost 4000 metres and several days trek or uncomfortable hours in a jeep from the nearest medical help. And I still had many things to see. I had brought every conceivable pill, potion and remedy to cover every possible illness or injury we may befall or encounter. I took every cold remedy in the bag and soldiered on.

After breakfast, we set out with Pradeep to see the three monasteries of Lo Manthang. As we had walked around and around inside Lo Manthang, we had passed a large red building that had several holes in its thick walls at about hip height. I put my eye to the holes but there was nothing but cold impenetrable darkness. I switched on the torch on my phone and poked my hand in through the gap, but its weak light was no match. Nothing could be seen, only a dark, brooding silence.

"I reckon that's it," I told Neville.

"Maybe."

One of the things I was determined to see in Lo Manthang was something that Michel Peissel had come upon in the darkness of one of the monasteries (after breaking in) and he had been awestruck. It was an enormous Buddha statue, fifty feet high, filling two storeys of the monastery. I told Pradeep.

"Ah yes. The Maitreya Buddha. Buddha who is to come."

"It's the really big one?"

"Yes. Very big," he assured me.

Pradeep, with Dipak quietly following, hands behind his back, led us through the main gate and, turning right, we went around into the narrow part of the 'L' shape that makes up Lo Manthang. We waited while a gate was unlocked for us then stepped into a building site. This part of the city houses the Dragkar-Thegchen Ling Gompa or monastery (also called just Chode Gompa) and the monastic school for eighty-three primary school aged monks. It suffered extensive damage in the earthquake. We picked our way around and over piles of dirt, rubble and stacks of new timber, while all around us was hammering and the whirr of a circular saw. Our guide, in his strangely high and constrained voice, pointed out a small hut made of plywood with a stove and some cooking pots inside.

"This one our temporary kitchen," he told us, and giggled.

"The other one was destroyed?"

"Ya. Other one destroyed and now we are building for student dining and kitchen."

He led us into the school courtyard where the sounds of building were now replaced by the chaotic sounds of a boys' school. Amongst the yelling and calling out we heard chanting. There didn't seem to be much supervision going on. There were boys running about in the courtyard, one was sweeping, but in at least one classroom boys sat at desks in maroon robes, their shaved heads bent over pages, droning in unison, but with no teacher in sight. They looked up with mild curiosity as we walked past the door and some called out Namaste.

"Look familiar?" I said to Neville.

On our first trip to Nepal, Neville and our boys volunteered at a school, ostensibly to teach English, but actually teaching anything or nothing or just supervising because a teacher had failed to turn up.

The calm silence inside the monastery assembly hall banished all outside noise. Here only dark quiet existed between high walls blackened from four centuries of incense and butter lamps. A large crack ran from the roof to the floor on one wall, caused by the earthquake. As in the other monasteries we had visited, two rows of low tables and stools faced each other where the monks sit to recite prayers. On each seat was a thick fur-lined cape ready for a young monk to burrow into for his early morning devotions. Paintings of the twenty-one "taras", the female incarnations of the Buddha, covered one wall.

"We believe the tara they protect us for good health and long life and from illness," our guide explained, "and every morning we have many students in here so they pray tara puja for their good health."

This "tara puja" is known as the Praises to the Twenty-One Taras when each of the names of taras and their individual mantras are read out. The two main taras are the green, from whom all other taras are said to have emanated, and the white one with her seven eyes, two in the usual place, one in the middle of her forehead and one for each hand and foot. The white tara is said to be the very essence of motherhood in her compassion and and kindness. It seems appropriate that the "mother" tara have eyes everywhere, especially when there are eighty-three small monks chanting below her. On another wall were paintings of the five Buddhas, green, red, white, yellow, and blue. They represent the five qualities of the Buddha and the aspiration to overcome ignorance, jealousy, pride, selfishness, and aggression. Pradeep told us they also represented the four points of the compass with white in the centre.

As we made our way out, the guide pointed to a thangka of the "wheel of life". The wheel is held as though in a violent struggle by the vicious-looking Yama, the god of death, with his bull's head, all sharp claws and bared fangs. In the centre are depictions of a pig, a snake, and a bird, each signifying ignorance, hatred or anger, and desire, the three things to overcome to achieve Dharma or Nirvana. In the wedges around these were pictures of how you may be reincarnated. If you don't get it right you may come back in the animal realm and live in complacent ignorance and suffer everything an animal does. If you return in the hungry ghost realm, you'll suffer constant craving which cannot be satisfied, hungry ghosts possessing a large empty stomach but narrow necks through which food cannot pass, turning to ashes in their mouths. Or you may end up in hell, a realm of fire and ice, suffering anger and terror, driving others away with your hatred and coldness, then, in your isolation, turning inwards and self-destructing.

Get it right and you'll make it to the realm of the gods, where you'll live with wealth, power and happiness, but your ignorance of suffering will probably mean you'll be reborn into a less desirable realm. You may come back to the realm of the Azuras, or jealous gods, but this probably won't work out either because you'll be hyper-competitive, paranoid of others getting the better of you and look down on everyone. The best realm to return to is the Human realm. Those in this realm are curious, questioning, and live with passion. They strive to explore, consume and acquire. But don't overdo the consuming or acquiring or you might end up back in one of the less desirable realms. The human realm is the only one from which you can finally be liberated from the wheel and achieve Dharma or Nirvana, but only if you work at it.

Now feeling slightly paranoid about how much ignorance, hatred, anger, or desire I was hanging onto, therefore putting myself at great risk for an unpleasant rebirth, we emerged into the sunlight and the guide locked the door. Next to the monastery was a small chorten with a photo attached. Our guide told us it contained the body of a lama.

"Also he was teacher of Dalai Lama," our guide said. "And he is also relative of Mustang king. He was pass away eleven years ago. At that time in Kathmandu there fall snow after sixty-two years, so we believe he is very powerful lama."

We followed the guide to another door, which he unlocked, and we were shown into the monastic museum. Far from the carefully curated artefacts, shielded by glass, that are seen in western museums, this was merely a room with stuff laid out on shelves and on the walls and floor. He pointed out old Bon texts, Bon being the religion that preceded

Buddhism, still practiced by some residents of Mustang and Tibet. I asked him if they were able to be read.

"We can read but cannot understand," he replied.

The books had been found in one of the many caves, but he said they had no idea how old they were. They simply sat on the shelf, unprotected, gathering dust with everything else.

There were instruments of torture, shackles, and swords from the days when battles were fought amongst the various small kingdoms. There were human bones, a flute made from an animal horn, and an enormous cooking pot.

"That's one big pot," I said.

"Ya, big pot," our guide replied. "Before in our monastery we have totally 600 monks. That when we use this pot. Now is useless," he said, and laughed.

There were also some elaborate masks and head dresses.

"These were the masks we use at the Tiji festival, but now we have new one," he told us. "Tiji festival, it is very famous here. Did you been?"

This festival, also known as "Tempa Chirim" draws hundreds of people every year. The festival goes for three days in late spring and is known as the "Chasing of the Demons". Lobas turn out in their finest clothes, monks dance in elaborate masks, offerings are made to appease the gods, and ancient muskets are fired, all extensively photographed and filmed by keen photographers perched on the rooftops overlooking the square. In fact the day Michel Peissel arrived in Lo Manthang this ceremony was in full swing.

This guide's work was now at an end and we thanked him and said goodbye, before following another man, a local artist, Tashi, who would now show us the other two monasteries. He carried a large torch.

"I have to bring big light, because inside is quite dark," he explained.

As we walked our new guide told us restoration work had been going on since 1999 funded by the American Himalayan Foundation.

"Every year, April to August, we work here," he said. "Our boss is from

Italy because mostly the Italians are the experts in restoration work. So they teach us, then we work together."

"But only in the summer because it's too cold in the winter?"

"Yah, but also the Nepal government give just four months permit for work here."

As we followed Tashi through the narrow streets, sparrows twittered in the warm autumn air, which was filled with the smell of dung and hay, but the city was quite empty. Only when we wandered about in the late afternoon did we see people, children coming home from school, some people carrying enormous loads of cut grass, so huge that only the lowest parts of a pair of legs could be seen, coming in from the harvest that was in full swing. At this time of day within the walls, only old men wandered, shuffling their prayer beads through their hands, while outside this ancient fortress, the wide barren land, even more ancient, stretched interminably in every direction, and, over all, a clear blue sky, flecked with moistureless clouds.

Tashi led us through an opening in a red wall and into a courtyard. Under the walkway that ran around above us, piles of timber were stacked untidily, some new, some old and broken. Rocks also littered the area; a blue tarp covered something next to a rough door opposite us. We followed Tashi up some stairs and onto the walkway above.

"This is the Jampa monastery," he explained. "Is the oldest one. Is from fourteenth century, so nearly six hundred years. Actually here we have three floor: ground floor, first floor, second, and now we can visit just the middle one."

He explained that it had been built by the second son of the first king of Mustang, Angen Szongbo. He unlocked a large padlock at the base of a heavy and intricately carved wooden door. The top of the doorway was scalloped with three arches and swirls were carved down either side. As he pushed it open the heavy creaking echoed a warning and we stepped into a cavernous hall.

Opposite, rising up out of the gloom below, was the great statue of the Maitreya Buddha, just as Peissel saw it in 1964, its golden face at the same time benevolent and forbidding. It demanded reverence. The middle floor was cut out around the Maitreya and the two smaller statues on either side—Manjushree, the god of wisdom, and Vajrapani, the god of protection—and was bordered by a railing. Made from clay, the Maitreya was entirely painted in gold. Tashi told us it was the tallest statue in Nepal. I was unable to take a photo, as in all the monasteries, but fortunately I have one picture taken by the photographer Thomas Laird, from the expedition he undertook with writer Peter Matthiessen in 1992, and which features in their book East of Lo Manthang, and the statue looked exactly the same. White silk katas hung from its raised fingers, thrown there by supplicants. I asked Tashi if they had needed to restore the statue, but he said they just cleaned it and added new paint to the face.

An altar sat against the railing in front of the statue with butter lamps and bowls of water, but there were also piles of rice, money, biscuits, a juice popper, and a cylinder of Pringles chips. A woman was placing offerings, lighting more lamps and sticks of incense, and offering prayers, just as others had done for six hundred years, probably in supplication for the same troubles and aspirations in their lives as she had in hers.

Leaning over the railing to one side, I peered down into the lower floor where the base of the statue sits, keen to see where Peissel had crept in fifty years before. Beyond the base, impenetrable darkness.

"What is in the lower floor?" I asked Tashi.

"Is just used for storage."

The thangkas hanging from the ceiling were blackened at the bottom, and we asked Tashi if they had been burnt in a fire.

"No burnt. Is old and just damaged. When we walk here we find just on the floor like rubbish, then we clean and we hang there so is safer."

"Why was it on the floor? Was this monastery not being used?"

"Oh, at that time the people doesn't know about the value of paintings. Also children came inside here and they are playing and throw the stone on the walls. So before 1999 all people of Lo Manthang they have no idea these are the important things."

I imagined people trampling on the artefacts in Westminster Abbey or Notre Dame, children throwing stones at the stained glass windows, but then, Notre Dame was trashed at various times and left to deteriorate.

In a place that in 2015 still had no access to modern health facilities, only a "health post" staffed by the equivalent of a paramedic, it seems hard to justify money being spent on restoring paintings in an ancient monastery. In Sienna Craig's book *Horses Like Lightning*, her friend Pushpa wondered if there was any point:

> The restoration projects will bring lots of foreign money and energy here, to protect and preserve these temples. They see them as 'world heritage' and there is truth in this perspective. The artwork is special. But meanwhile any young Loba with the means to do so is leaving Mustang to forge a life elsewhere, and all the local people with money invest in business abroad or property in Kathmandu. Nobody invests much in Mustang these days. They expect foreigners to do it. If it weren't so sad, it would be funny.

As we explored the monasteries of Tibet during our 2019 trip, Tenzin explained how the people help to maintain them, painting them every year, renewing the floors by tamping down the mixture used, singing as they work. I told him of how the monasteries in Mustang had been left to deteriorate and that it was only through foreign efforts they were now being restored.

"Well," he said, "I heard it from a Sherpa that that area is cursed."

It's easier to imagine Tibet is cursed. Almost all of the monasteries in Tibet were destroyed during the Cultural Revolution, but in the early 1980s the Chinese government had a change of heart and the Tibetans were allowed to rebuild them. Perhaps having to fight for their culture and religion makes the Tibetans more fiercely care for and guard their monasteries. Unlike the people of Lo, they cannot leave and invest abroad. Why stay home and restore centuries old buildings and paintings when you have the freedom to explore other things that might make life worth living?

I try to imagine it from a Catholic perspective. Catholicism isn't just the religion in which I was raised, it encompasses a whole lot of cultural traditions and references going back to my family having originally come from Ireland. My mother still remembered her Irish grandparents. Her mother would have grown up with an Irish perspective on many things. My mother gave me her book of Irish fairy tales. And though I've only visited Ireland once and I'm many generations removed from it, there is a perplexing nostalgia that creeps into my heart when I hear Irish music.

And while I still practice as a Catholic, I don't think I'd be too worried about the local cathedral falling into ruins. Unless, that is, I was imprisoned in my country and my cultural identity was threatened by the invading culture. If China were to invade Australia and tear down all Catholic churches and my children were forced to learn only Mandarin and we were forbidden to practice our religion would I cling more fiercely to it?

Perhaps the curse that has fallen on Mustang is that in 1992 it was opened up to the outside world. The lure of more money and opportunity and a more comfortable way of life has made the need to practice religion and maintain its symbols redundant.

Fifty-four mandalas covered the walls and were in varying states of repair. Tashi told us there were fifty-four more on the floor above, 108 in all, the sacred number in Tibetan Buddhism. The black soot from centuries of butter lamps and incense had been cleaned off, a process that took about six years. Butter made from vegetable oil is now used for the lamps instead of animal butter as it doesn't give off black smoke.

"Paintings are much damaged from water leakage, because in winter snow, summer rain, and before 1999, before the project, people doesn't care the monastery," Tashi explained.

Streaks ran down and across the paintings from the high ceiling. He also told us that the earthquake had caused the paintings to detach from the wall. He knocked on the wall and it made a hollow sound.

"So next year we have to fix again. We have to make a hole and inject by syringe, put glue inside then put the paintings back."

Many of the paintings were still in very bad condition. I wondered if they would ever be able to completely restore the monastery before having to start again.

I asked Tashi what was on the third floor above us.

"That is like a Mahakala room, so is a tantric [religious] room, so nobody can go inside. So in the year just one time there is a big puja. At that time we can go and visit, otherwise all year closed."

Mahakala is a fierce protector god and the fear was real. It would be easy to dismiss these fears. I imagined pushing open the upper door and finding just another dimly lit, dusty old room, but how can I know for sure there would be no repercussions for opening up this room at an inappropriate time? Tenzin told me Tibet, unlike Nepal, had never been hit by an earthquake because it was protected by a god which sat on the joints of a demon positioned around the land, preventing them from flexing and causing earthquakes. He also believed he and his wife has been unable to have children because one or both of them must be carrying some bad karma.

As in all the monasteries and lodges there was a photo of the Dalai Lama on the altar. Neville asked if he'd ever visited Lo Manthang.

"No, he never came here. He never came to Nepal also, because the Nepal government can't give protection, because it's near from China. So just we keep his photo," he explained, and laughed.

Tashi led us out into the sunshine and pulled the ancient heavy doors closed and, with a jangling of keys and padlock, firmly locked them, leaving the Maitreya and its fifty-four mandalas to continue to sit silently in the darkness, eternal guardians of Lo Manthang and its Buddhist faith.

The spell broke in the light outside. We were out of the awe-inspiring presence of the enormous statue, safe now from its forbidding presence and that of the literally thousands of painted buddha images. For 600 years, through all of European history in that time, all the wars, all the advances in science and technology, the explorations of Earth and space, famines, rising and falling of rulers and governments, even earthquakes, that statue, that image of a being believed to be coming in the future, has sat alone in silence and darkness, in a temple on a plateau in the midst of a mountainous, rocky desert, unyielding to time, waiting. I took some strange comfort in this fact. I can imagine that if I lived in Lo Manthang, I could go and sit with this unchanging thing, knowing that whatever happened in my life I could always return and sit in its forbidding but benevolent presence.

Tashi led us in a kora around the outside of the middle storey, explaining as we went that this is was a form of prayer, much like spinning a prayer wheel, before leading us to the Tubchen monastery.

This monastery and the Jampa monastery were the two large red buildings that could be seen rising above the walls and all other buildings of Lo Manthang. We entered through a heavy wooden door and took three steps down into a small porch. The floor level of the monastery, Tashi explained, had sunk overtime, below the ground level of Lo Manthang, due to centuries of weather and the piling of more layers of mud onto the roof to try to seal it. As a result the ceiling was thought to have weighed some 200 tons, putting enormous pressure on the joists and pillars and causing shifting and cracking. Since the restoration began, this ceiling had been removed and replaced using traditional methods. The sinking and the rising damp also meant that the lower parts of many paintings had been completely lost, literally falling off the wall as they were painted onto a surface that is attached to the wall. Strange to think that while Michelangelo was painting the Sistine chapel, artists were at work in the Tubchen monastery using the same techniques.

The art restorers from Italy did not believe they should repaint the lost parts, feeling it was more historically authentic to simply restore what was still there. But the painting and statues in the monasteries are not simply artistic representations of the deities, but living deities themselves and to leave them incomplete was unthinkable; people could not conceive of praying before incomplete gods. So for the previous four years they had been resurfacing the walls and now, having drawn all the outlines, they were ready to add colour. Large cracks ran the length of the walls of this monastery as well, but, Tashi explained, they were not caused by the earthquake, it just made them worse.

Above the door wires ran to a small, naked, fluorescent bulb hanging above the entry porch. It had been installed only in the last couple of weeks, since the installation of the solar plant. Tashi explained that Tubchen had been built in the fifteenth century by the third king of Mustang, Tashi Gon. While the door itself was quite plain, the surrounding doorway was intricately carved albeit somewhat worn. Above the lintel were six carved wooden snow lions. The snow lion is a mythical creature of the Himalayas symbolising fearlessness and youthful joy. They had fierce, pointed canine teeth, pointed raised tongues, as though roaring, and front paws raised in defiance.

"That is a kind of ancient animal," Tashi told us, "like a dinosaur. Now we cannot find. Before we have in mountains. Is all totally white."

We entered an anteroom where a small fuse box and switch were attached to a pillar. Four large statues sat, two on each side, guardians of the temple. Our voices echoed and again, all sound from outside was gone. We now entered what I can only describe as a vast cathedral. Great pillars, thirty-five of them, the width of whole tree trunks held up the roof, almost eight metres high. The brackets atop the pillars were intricately carved and around the edge of the skylight recess were more snow lions. This was also the place where meetings were held. For years, before the restoration work began, it sat completely unused, an old woman just lighting the butter lamps each day. Tashi showed us on one wall paintings of the eight Boddhisatvas, those beings which have attained enlightenment, each with their two attendants. On another wall were paintings of the five buddhas—green, red, yellow, blue, white—with the thousand buddhas in the background, the number of fully enlightened buddhas who will exist in this time period. We are living in what is known as the Fortunate Aeon; how many years that is is never specified. In the next Aeon, the Maitreya Buddha will come.

As well as their respective colours they were also painted with gold. It had taken twenty-five people working four months a year for four years, after cleaning, restoring the surface of the walls, and drawing the outlines, to get to the point where they could begin to paint. At this point they looked like a colour-by-numbers picture—drawings with blocks of colour filling the spaces in between the lines. When this was done, they would add the intricate detail.

Along the back wall were huge statues, some made from clay, but others all of copper. Katas hung from them and butter lamps glowed along the altar in front, which, like Jampa, was covered in offerings. Dim light streamed from the skylight above. Tashi pointed to the right side where one of the statues was missing.

"Two hundred years ago there was a big earthquake and the north wall completely falling down and we lost one statue from there and also the monastery became smaller."

A completely new wall had been built in its place, but whether they would ever get around to painting it after all the restoration work, he didn't know.

There was a photo of a young boy monk whom Tashi told us was the youngest son of the Prince of Mustang. He was a new incarnate lama. Having finished primary school at the monastery in Lo Manthang he was now at a high school in India. He was destined to become head of the monasteries of Lo Manthang. There was also the same photo we had seen in all the other monasteries—Sakya Trinzin, head of the Sakya sect. On the left side of the altar was a large high chair, which, Tashi said, belongs to him and no one else can sit in it.

"So does he come and visit these monasteries?" I asked.

"Actually last year he came here for three hours by helicopter," Tashi replied. "Also is danger from Chinese so is difficult to came here. So finally we got last year that chance."

"But if he came here what could the Chinese do?"

"Because he is Tibetan citizen he is in danger."

"So would they actually come here and arrest him?"

Tashi laughed. "Ya ya ya! That's a problem."

"They would actually come here and arrest him and take him back to China?"

"Ya ya. Because the Chinese is very strong, so is a danger. So before we is careful. Is better."

"And that's why the Dalai Lama doesn't come here either?"

"Ya. So people from our region, they go to India to meet him."

"How come the Chinese can come here if it's Nepal?"

I could see Tashi becoming nervous but I wanted to understand how the Chinese could so easily access and interfere in a bordering country.

"Because this is free border. They can came here any times. We cannot stop because we are very small country. Chinese are very big and very powerful and very rich. Everything they have."

"Does that worry people here?"

"For us? No problem. But for high lama, we careful. For us is good, yeah? They help us many things."

"Like the solar plant."

"Ya, solar plant. Before they give us also some foods."

"Why do they do that?"

"Because we are poor country, they are rich country so they can help us." And he laughed, but his laugh had taken on a nervous tone.

Unfortunately, China does not give aid to Nepal out of the goodness of their heart in Mustang or anywhere else. Residents of the village of Samdzong, now relocated further south due to dwindling water supply, had reported the Chinese inspecting their homes and ordering them to take down pictures of the Dalai Lama in exchange for food aid. They fear growing Chinese influence in the area may lead to them suffering the same fate as Tibet. Sienna Craig told me she believes it extremely unlikely that China would actually take over Upper Mustang but that they certainly have serious influence in the area, politically and economically. The Nepalese government is under enormous pressure from the Chinese to control the activities of Tibetan refugees and any expression of their culture in exchange for aid. There are rumours of Chinese spies looking for Tibetan defectors.

And while the Dalai Lama cannot visit Nepal in fear for his safety, the people of Mustang are free (with the exception, perhaps, of those living close to the border) to display his picture as we saw in the lodges. They are also free, if they have the means, to visit him. But over the border, just twenty kilometres away, the Tibetans are forbidden any mention of the Dalai Lama.

On our journey through Tibet we visited the Ganden Monastery outside Lhasa. After touring inside the monastery we made a clockwise walk, a kora, around the mountain. On the bare grassy hillside we stopped to rest and so Tenzin could have a cigarette. "My bad habit," he apologised.

As we were out of earshot and sight of anyone else, I asked Tenzin if he would like to see my pictures of Mustang. He sat down beside me and gazed eagerly at the photos exclaiming, "This is Tibet!" It was as though he were looking back in time to the Tibet that was lost before he was even born. I showed him a picture of the inside of the stupa in Kagbeni and when he saw the picture of the Dalai Lama his voice dropped to a whisper. "Oh! Dalai Lama!"

The Dalai Lama's is the only photo never seen in any of the monasteries in Tibet. His predecessor (or previous incarnation) the thirteenth Dalai Lama is pictured, as are the Karmapa Lama, the now defunct Lamdring Lama, and the controversial eleventh Panchen Lama, appointed by the Chinese, replacing the one chosen by the Dalai Lama. (That original

Panchen Lama remains missing.) When we visited the Potala Palace, Tenzin was allowed to refer to him as the fourteenth Dalai Lama when we viewed his former living quarters, but there were no pictures.

"If I ever get a passport," said Tenzin, "I will go to Mustang."

When I later mentioned the Chinese were planning to build a road from the Tibetan border down through Mustang, Tenzin said, "Then the Chinese will see the real Tibet."

But what is the real Tibet?

Mustang is Mustang and it is Nepal and it is Tibetan, but it is not Tibet. Just as my home, the home I grew up in is not home any more. And yet I still think of it as home. It's where I come from and every inch of it is familiar to me and yet it has changed. The house I knew has been renovated. Two of my sisters have been to see it, asked the new owner if they could look inside, but I don't want to. I want to remember home as it was.

If Tenzin went searching for Tibet in Mustang I fear he would be disappointed. Many things would be familiar but others different. Even the language; it is a dialect of Tibetan. Mustang as it was, and Tibet as it was, are gradually disappearing, swept away like the sands of the mandala.

CHAPTER 16

To See Tibet

Dervla Murphy wrote in her book *The Waiting Land* about her frustration at being so close to the Tibetan border whilst trekking north of Kathmandu in 1965, but not being allowed to cross. In 1924 Alexandra David-Neel risked everything, dressed as a Tibetan pilgrim, to become the first western woman to make it to Lhasa. Susie Carson Rijnhart, a Canadian doctor and missionary, and her husband, set out for Lhasa in 1898 with their baby son, but their son died and her husband disappeared, presumed murdered, leaving Susie and their staff to flee back to China. Many others tried but were discovered and escorted back over the border or died of starvation and cold. I knew I couldn't cross the border, but when I found myself just twelve kilometres away I knew I had to at least get close.

I was on my second visit to Nepal in 2013 and I had come to a place called The Last Resort, a place for people to bungy jump from the high suspension bridge if they are so inclined, or to get out of the chaos of Kathmandu and relax in the mountains for a weekend. We stayed at The Last Resort on our first trip to Nepal and two of our sons had gone bungy-jumping, the youngest not being big enough, much to his disappointment. As we were so close to Tibet, I decided I wanted to travel that tiny bit further just to see it.

"No I don't want to go," Neville said. "What's the point? I'm not cramming onto one of those buses packed with people and goats just to see the border."

I could have gone alone, but being with my family, I felt like I couldn't just strike out on my own. I was part of the family unit, a mother, not Rose the intrepid adventurer. Neville wouldn't have cared, he just couldn't see the point in sitting in a bus for half the day just to see more of the same. So I didn't go, and regretted it.

So when I made the same trip with my friend Kirsten and found myself with another opportunity, I wasn't going to miss out a second time. Kirsten was a seasoned traveller in Asia who had driven enough terrifying, high, narrow roads to refuse to accompany me on another one just to peer over the border into Tibet.

"But the road isn't made," she argued when I tried to talk her into coming.

"But it's probably no worse than it was heading up this far," I replied.

In the end, I couldn't persuade her so she stayed behind and decided she would rather climb down to the rushing Bhote Kosi river and put her feet in the icy water while I braved the unmade road. I asked the guy in charge of the tours up to the Resort how I might get to the border.

"There's a bus that goes every hour," he told me.

"That's a local bus isn't it?" He nodded.

We'd seen these buses on the way up, people packed in tight, more people and sometimes their animals on the roof. These buses frequently fell off the mountain roads into the ravines below due to bad driving and poor maintenance.

"Would you travel up that road in one of those?"

"No," he admitted, "but for 3500 rupees our bus can take you." About forty dollars. Done.

So after all the day-trippers had been dropped off I followed the driver and his young assistant back over the high bridge.

"Goodbye Gulaph!" called Kirsten from the front porch of our tent below, as though she might never see me again. (Gulaph is Nepali for Rose).

I took the front seat next to the driver and we set off. The road was no worse than the stretch before The Last Resort, but the scenery was beautiful. Waterfalls fell down the steep mountain sides, cascading through pools that made me want to jump in and rinse off the dust and filth of Kathmandu. We sped on through villages where shops filled with garishly-coloured clothes, piles of florescent synthetic blankets, plastic things, pots, pans, and rice-cookers lined the road. We had to stop a couple of times at police checkpoints. At one, a police officer leaned in the driver's window and, glancing at me, appeared to question the driver. The one word I recognised was "border". I imagined the conversation went like:

Police: Where are you headed?
Driver: I'm taking this white woman up to the border.
Police: What does she want to go up there for?
Driver: Beats me, but she's paying me so I don't care.
Police: (Glancing suspiciously at me) Hmmm. Ok then.

And on we went

After about forty minutes we reached Kodari where we stopped and the driver reversed the bus up to park next to some trucks. The driver's assistant pointed onwards up the road saying,

"Border, ten minutes walk."

I looked around. There were a lot of people in this bustling village, not one of them was white and a lot of them were staring at me. Ok, I thought, I'm brave and adventurous, I'll be ok, and I set off up to the Chinese border. I then realised the young man was coming with me and I sighed with relief. He led me up the busy road, lined on the river side with shops and dingy cafes and two-storey dwellings painted blue and white with a balcony along the second floor. The people were more

Tibetan looking here than in Kathmandu, round faces with wide-set eyes and full red cheeks. Men and women struggled along, bent forward under huge loads strapped around their foreheads. As one woman came towards me I saw that her eyes were inflamed and swollen. The right was worse than the left and she dabbed at it with a filthy cloth as she walked. I saw an old man leading his equally old wife, both shuffling with difficulty up the road.

As we came closer to the border we had to weave our way between trucks queued up to cross the so-called "Friendship Bridge" between the two countries. My guide led me through and we emerged onto the bridge.

"China," he announced, pointing.

So I brought my camera up and took a photo. Instantly, at least five men came running towards me.

"No photos! No photos!" they called frantically.

As they surrounded me I said, "Ok, ok, I'm deleting it, I'm deleting it," quickly pressing buttons trying to remember how to delete a photo. "See? It's gone," and I showed them.

They all looked ridiculously relieved. I later found out some of these were likely plain-clothes Chinese police.

"This is bad country," said one man quietly, after they'd left me alone. "Big trouble with this country."

Strangely, the whole thing felt staged, as though no trip to the Chinese border should be without incident. My guide then led me down and alongside the bridge.

"Now you take photo," he said. And I did. Nothing happened.

There really wasn't much to see but that wasn't the point. I was happy knowing I had gone as far as I could. Perched on the opposite cliff, high above the river, a grey, Soviet-looking building spread itself, plain, square windows, gazing blankly back at Nepal. A large sign formed part of the wall and read: Welcome to the People's Republic of China. Nothing about the whole place was welcoming. I wondered what went on in that building.

The road into Tibet zig-zagged up the mountain rising behind it and disappeared into a part of the world that for centuries was made inaccessible by the Tibetans themselves, and is now only accessible with the most stringent and oppressive restrictions imposed by the Chinese.

The 2013 documentary, *Bringing Tibet Home*, tells the story of the artist Tenzing Rigdol's art installation "Our Land Our People". Rigdol decided to bring 20,000 kilograms of soil from Tibet to the exiled community in Dharamsala in India so the Tibetan people could once again walk on their home soil. The film tells the story of this pain-staking undertaking. In a scene reminiscent of my own encounter, the Chinese refused to allow the truck carrying the soil to cross the border at Kodari so it was instead taken bag by small bag by secret zip-line across the border further downstream and loaded onto a waiting truck there. The whole fraught operation took weeks, much of it spent by Rigdol sitting in Kathmandu not knowing what was happening. But the result was worth it. The out-pouring of emotion was enormous as the Tibetan people in Dharamsala walked on their home soil, some for the first time in more than fifty years, some, like the children, for the first time ever. When the time came to dismantle the installation it was given over to the people. They brought whatever containers they had and filled them with the precious soil so they could forever keep something of home.

On one of my last visits home, when I knew it wouldn't be there much longer, I took a cutting of the magnolia tree that grew next to the side steps. I loved its beautiful maroon and white flowers and loved the thought of a plant from this same tree blooming outside my new home. Alas, the cutting died, but I wish I had something, even a container of soil from the yard at home in Bellingen. I can feel in my own heart how those exiled Tibetans felt at being able to possess a piece of their beloved, lost home.

Twice on the way back we were stopped at checkpoints and police boarded the bus, thoroughly searching each empty seat. A Tibetan-looking girl, who seemed to be known to the driver, got on at one point.

The police made her open all the plastic shopping bags she had with her. When I later asked our host mother, about this she said that a lot of smuggling went on over the border.

"And I guess they were looking for Tibetan refugees?" I asked

She shrugged her shoulders.

In Tibet, I mentioned the incident to Tenzin and asked him what he thought they were looking for.

"Tibetans," he replied.

The town of Kodari was destroyed by the 2015 earthquake. The imposing Chinese buildings and the small wooden Nepalese buildings all crumbled and fell into the gorge below. Tenzin told me the people living in Dram, the village on the Tibetan side had to move to Shigatse after the earthquake and that many of the old people died for they were unable to adjust to the higher altitude.

CHAPTER 17

Out of Sight

On our next night in Lo Manthang, during our pre-dinner drinks, I asked Pradeep about another form of burial which I'd read about in Michel Peissel's book. Peissel writes that during his stay in Lo Manthang, he noticed *Om Mane Padme Hum* inscribed on a rectangular patch of wall above where he slept. His friend Pemba calmly told him that was where his brother was buried, within the wall of the house. Peissel pointed to another area and was told another brother was buried there. I asked Pradeep if the Lobas still practiced this form of burial. He made a face and said he'd never heard of it before, so he asked the owner of the lodge, who told him it was indeed true.

If a male died without having any grandsons, or if his sons died before having sons, they were wrapped in salt and buried in the wall of the family home.

In Tibet I asked Tenzin if he had ever heard of this fifth form of corpse disposal, but he had never heard of it either. I checked with Sienna Craig who told me that a man who has died without producing a son, is still considered part of the household and therefore needs to be kept within the house to prevent "negative impacts". Michel Peissel's companion,

Pemba, called these negative impacts "ghosts". When and if a grandson is born into the family, these members are then removed and disposed of.

The King and Queen of Mustang had just one child, a boy, who died at the age of eight. They adopted their nephew who became their heir, but presumably their young son is buried somewhere in the walls of the palace.

If my family were from Lo Manthang, when David died, he would have been interred in the walls of our house instead of lying in the cold blue-tiled grave (although it seems Rose would still have been laid to rest there, alone). As a mother, I can't imagine how hard it would be to turn around, walk away, and leave your baby to lie alone in the dark and cold of a cemetery. I can fully understand how comforting it would be to have their little body close by, actually part of the home, still part of the family and its day-to-day life. As the parent, I think you would still have the feeling of being able to protect the child. They would literally be in the in-between space, not inside the house with the living, but not out somewhere alone and vulnerable. Being inside the wall itself they are at once a part of, but separate. An adult has lived and has therefore had some time to prepare for or contemplate death. A child has only just begun and is therefore not yet equipped for the unknown and possible dangers associated with the world of the dead. Then, once you die, the child can be taken out and let go, now having a parent in the realm of the dead to be with them. Or perhaps at this point they are safe to be reincarnated.

Because of my cold Pradeep suggested maybe we should stay on in Lo Manthang for longer so I could rest, and head straight back from there instead of taking the planned side trip to Yara and Luri Gompa. I was determined that this wasn't going to happen. It was quite unlikely that I would ever return to Mustang so I was going to see as much as I could unless completely incapacitated. So I declined this suggestion and told him I'd be fine and retired to my bed early in the hope that the next day I'd feel better. He kindly produced a tiny bottle of something called Sancho, a special blend of Himalayan essential oils that smelt like menthol, saying it would help. It certainly cleared my nose.

I have reflected on Pradeep's suggestion since then. I wondered whether he didn't want to go to Luri Gompa and was using my cold as an excuse. It also made me feel, once again, that none of them, Pradeep, Dipak or Abhinav, thought me up to the journey and didn't want to be stuck in the middle of nowhere with an ailing female.

It sometimes annoyed me when Dipak or Abhinav rushed up and grabbed control of my horse. There was a moment when Dipak took hold of the bridle strap but I still had the reins. Since he obviously wanted to take control I let the reins go.

"Take it! Take it!" he barked at me, and I obediently took them up again. It made me feel stupid. It was the only time Dipak showed anything like annoyance.

Black flies got into our room every day and buzzed against the windows until dark when they mysteriously disappeared. The evenings were becoming quite cool now—enough for a down jacket and beanie in the evenings—but the thick earth and stone walls meant that by morning it felt like the heating had been left on.

That night I lay within the protection of those stone walls, warm in my sleeping bag, and listened to the voices outside our room, speaking in a language I didn't understand. It was hard to grasp how far from home I was, whatever home was for me now, since what I had always called home had vanished. I had a home, but it would never be permanent. And in fact, as much as I loved that home, a beautiful old Queenslander in the bush, I was conscious of never becoming too attached to it. I knew we were just another of the countless families that have occupied it over its more than one hundred years. It wasn't really mine and never would be.

I lay there hoping I wouldn't become really sick, remembering our first trip to Nepal. By the time we finished our month of volunteering I had a cold that time too. We took the bus to Pokhara, but by the fourth night there I knew I had a chest infection. I started the antibiotics I had brought with me and the next day we caught a bus to Chitwan National Park, a jungle down on the flat lands of the terai. After five jolting hours and subjected to the constant jarring sound of Indian singing we arrived at our very basic hotel. We were scheduled to head straight out on some adventure, but I was too sick by then. Instead I lay in bed and listened in wonder at the sound of elephants trumpeting in the distance while Neville took the boys out bike-riding. And I cried.

By evening I felt worse. Neville called the volunteer agency to ask what medical facilities were available in the area in case I needed to see a doctor. There were none. I would have to catch the bus back to Kathmandu the following day, or if it was really urgent, charter a plane.

I felt terrified and I felt angry. Here I was, sick, with no help if things were getting worse, but worse, here I was in the Nepalese jungle and I was laid up in bed. What happened next is hard to understand and open to interpretation, but at the very moment I felt the most afraid I saw a woman with dark, curly hair, her features indistinct, and behind her, more women, looking at me and laughing. I felt, more than heard a voice say, "Did you really think we would leave you alone here when you're sick?" I was startled into an overwhelming feeling of relief. I felt surrounded by love. It was as though it emanated from all the women in my life: my female friends, my sisters, the women in my life who had died, all of them. And I knew in that moment I was going to be ok. And I cried again.

I've often reflected on that experience in the years since. I had never had such an experience before, but then I'd never found myself sick far from medical care before. I wonder when we are in a situation that is less crowded, when life is pared back to the necessities and the modern world has receded, whether we become more receptive to what else is around us, unseen but powerful.

CHAPTER 18

One Last Night With the Russians

That afternoon we went for a final walk around Lo Manthang. People sat in the late afternoon sun, as though soaking it up while they could, for it would soon be winter. Some called "Namaste", one older man "Tashi Delek" the Tibetan greeting. Men carrying loads of hay and heavy feed bags strapped to their foreheads walked with purpose. Somewhere a goat bleated. In one street, children, still in their school uniforms, called out "Where are you from?" and, a common greeting, "Where are you going?".

Old women sat on the ground, backs against the wall, chatting. Men sat on ledges outside shops desultorily twirling small prayer wheels, asking, "You like to look in my shop?"

One elderly man, whom we had seen a few times on our walks, offered "Rooftop view?", and we had seen a few photographers take up his offer. Of course there would be a fee for this privilege.

Women, bent double, swept leaves from the rough ground with the small brooms made from sticks tied together. Others crouched by taps washing clothes and metal dishes. Goat hides lay spread out, drying. The air was crisp with the chill of the coming night and, as ever, the smell of manure, clods of it drying along the ledges, was everywhere. Around this ancient, walled city, the ageless hills rose, silently, imperiously, in the quiet understanding that this city, which had stood for nearly 700 years on its "Plain of Aspiration", would one day be gone.

Outside the city walls, a large square building with square towers on each corner was being constructed, two storeys high, three at the corners. The bottom storey and the top of each tower had an outer surface of stones while the other walls were smoothly rendered. An "R" had been worked into the stonework on at least one of the towers. It had timber windows set deep into the cement grey wall. Large sheets of plywood covered what looked like the main entrance. It was still very much a construction site but no work was going on. This was a new boutique hotel being built by the royal family but I suspected earthquake reconstruction had taken priority, especially repair of the palace, since the King and Queen could not return to Lo Manthang until it was made safe. A boutique hotel seemed incongruous in Lo Manthang. It's not the kind of destination you'd head for if you wanted luxury accommodation. I thought of this half-built luxury hotel later when we were in Tsarang and I overheard a French woman anxiously asking their guide whether he knew yet which lodge they were staying at in Lo Manthang saying, "is it a good one?" as though the hotels of Upper Mustang had a star rating guide.

Outside, between the Kunga Shopping Shop and the Lo Manthang Youth Club, advertising "hot showers" in hand-painted letters on its wall, two women and their children squatted by the stream washing clothes. Here the stream was wider just before the concrete channel began that directed the water around and through the main gate, and channeled it through the whole city. It ran clear and shallow over smooth stones. Using bars of soap and plastic scrubbing brushes, the women scrubbed the clothing on the larger stones. Even the children's shoes were waiting in the queue to be cleaned. Two little girls called out "Namaste" and one proudly pointed to one of the women, saying, "this my mother!"

We passed a boy of about six trying to ride a small broken bike, its back wheel hopelessly buckled. We watched three little boys of about four pulling two cardboard boxes along by pieces of string. Every now and then they stopped to put some leaves or bits of rubbish in the boxes, then continued on, chatting seriously about the whole operation.

As we rounded a corner on the outside of the wall, a window opened in one of the lodges and a voice called, "Hullo Australia!" It was the large Russian man. That night, he and his two female companions joined us at dinner, apparently because ours was the only lodge serving meat. I don't know what meat they found because we didn't find any. We drank Kukri rum with Pradeep and they became very merry drinking Lhasa beer. The one woman who could speak English told us they were from St. Petersburg. I was ridiculously fascinated by the fact that here were living, breathing people whose everyday lives were conducted in St. Petersburg, where the characters of Gogol's and Dostoyevsky's stories had paraded along the Nevsky Prospect and the doomed Romanov's had wandered the countless rooms of their Winter Palace, oblivious of their fate.

"How cold is it there in winter," I asked the woman, indulging my fascination for places of extreme cold.

"It didn't even snow there last winter," she replied with grim resignation.

The man sat beaming with a slightly drunken boyish grin, his big frame slouching awkwardly. The woman told us they were taking the jeep back to Jomsom the next day, but that she wondered how her friend would fit comfortably into the vehicle.

"Yes," said Pradeep. "Is like trying to fit elephant into the jeep."

We all laughed as much at the image this conjured but more at the fact that what Pradeep had said was vaguely insulting. The Russian man just shrugged his shoulders. No one seemed to be offended, but as though to make up for his potentially insulting remark, Pradeep added,

"But you can move faster. Mouse, he go 'neep, neep'," and Pradeep ran his fingers along the table like a mouse. "But elephant, 'lomp, lomp', " and he put one shoulder in front the other. How much the man understood, I don't know, but he seemed to take it well.

His friend also told us they had paid a jeep to take them up to the border that day to take photos.

"They pay 3000 rupees for jeep to take them to the border," said Pradeep later. "Why? There is nothing to see!"

I didn't tell him that I had once done the same.

That night, our last in Lo Manthang, I climbed up the ladder at the end of the upstairs balcony and onto the roof. The moon was up and the hills glowed pale orange and butter yellow in the last remnant of daylight. Prayer flags fluttered in the breeze and birds still twittered busily. Over the wall, the palace stood dark and abandoned. In the distance a horn blared, then a tractor with a large trailer attached, heavily laden with green grass, rattled noisily up the street, pausing briefly with each gear change, like an old man catching his breath, and carrying with it the jarring sound of Nepali pop music.

CHAPTER 19

To Dhe

Next morning as we stood waiting in the dining room, ready to leave, we heard the hollow jangle of goat bells. I leant on one of the benches and pushed open the window. The smell of goat, like the sweet smell of rotting meat, rose from the street below. The shepherd followed, wearing jeans and a khaki army camouflage jacket, a small canvas bag slung over his shoulder. They passed Abhinav who was saddling my horse. Then Pradeep stuck his head in the doorway to say it was time.

And so we ambled out of Lo Manthang. I had seen it and was a tiny bit sad knowing I would never see it again, because I knew I would never make that journey again. The thing that gave me the energy to get there was the excitement of discovery. And anyway, I could see it would not remain as it was forever. I now saw it like a sandcastle but with a solid core. The wind would gradually blow away the sand, but the essence of Lo Manthang—its monasteries, some of its culture, some of its people—would remain; no longer the once thriving fortress town on a vibrant trade route, with its own royal family, but still an awe-inspiring, beautiful place, worth seeing if only to be reminded of how life once was.

I envied Michel Peissel, who really did find a place untouched by time. Back then, in the 1960s, the people of Lo had only the vaguest idea that other countries existed. In Peissel's book is a map of the world as it was described to him by the then king, the father of the last king. Lhasa was considered to be the centre of the world, and judging by the fact that there was a panorama of Lhasa on the wall of every lodge we visited, in the hearts of the Lobas, it still is. The world as they conceived it was a half-disc, surrounded by water. Nepal, China, and India were situated on the disc, but the other countries they had heard of—Japan, America, England—were islands floating somewhere around it.

And in my heart, my own home, as I knew it, its own core, would always exist. There it could remain untouched. When I close my eyes, I can put myself right back there. I can hear my father come in the back door, my mother in the kitchen, the sound of the kitchen door opening and closing, the smell of the orange trees in the yard, the smell of ether in my father's surgery. And I feel safe, even though, in reality, I wasn't. I was always alone.

We climbed to the top of the Lo La, the pass above Lo Manthang, and, after stopping for a last look back at the walled city, we headed on to our next destination: Yara. Then my phone pinged for the first time in days, a text from my son Tom:

"The car isn't starting any more and the upstairs shower is stuffed. Also I need shoes for my formal so can you transfer some money?"

A reminder that while I was braving the perils of the Tibetan plateau, normal life would be waiting for me when I returned home.

The other seventeen-year-old, travelling with us, had been largely unseen while we were in Lo Manthang, except when I saw him watching movies on a laptop downstairs in the lodge, or sitting on the ledge outside trying to hide his cigarettes from me. However, Abhinav had also been shopping and had acquired a small portable speaker, decorated with the minions from the movie Despicable Me, that had been loaded with modern Nepali music. So where usually we travelled in relative silence, with just the sound of the wind, rushing water, the horse bells, the distant bleating of sheep and goats, we were now treated to tinny blaring music from the speaker which hung by a strap from his wrist. He grinned, looking very pleased with himself, which was a change from the bored, disgruntled look he often wore.

"He paid one thousand rupees for that," Pradeep told us, shaking his head, when, the following day, Abhinav sat tapping and shaking the thing in frustration as it kept repeating the same passage of music.

We were heading south again but would soon turn east and cross the Kali Gandaki. We followed a rough track of loose, sandy soil along a ridge. As we ambled along I found myself looking down at the horse and footprints in the sand made by other travellers, not thinking about much at all, until I realised that I was no longer seeing just horse and human footprints but also large paw prints. They were heading in the opposite direction, back to Lo Manthang. I turned around to Dipak and Abhinav walking behind me and holding my hand in a claw shape, shook it towards to the ground. Dipak immediately ran up thinking I wanted to get off the horse.

"No," I said. "Paw prints," and pointed at the ground.

"Ya," replied Dipak.

"Snow leopard?"

"Ya, ya. Big one," he replied, and laughed.

My eyes were now glued to the ground and the prints continued until we reached the turnoff to Yara, where they gave way to small goat or sheep prints. They continued along the track that led to Tsarang, not far from Marong, where 120 goats had been killed by a leopard just a couple of weeks before. We now turned to descend towards the river, but the horses decided they'd rather not. The brown horse, carrying the packs, took off running sideways off the track. Abhinav set off yelling abuse and throwing rocks at it, trying to steer it back onto the track. Meanwhile, Dipak motioned to me to dismount because the descent was too steep and slippery for riding. Let go, my white horse took off too, and try as they might, Abhinav and Dipak could not get it back. It turned and took off back to Lo Manthang; it had clearly enjoyed its time there and decided it would prefer to return. The brown horse tried to follow it, but Dipak managed to stop it in time. It kept stopping and trying to turn but we all managed to keep it going in the right direction. Dipak turned and ran back up to help Abhinav.

We were a long way down when we finally spied Dipak far above us walking down alone. There was no sign of Abhinav or the other horse, so we all just carried on, slipping and gingerly making our way down the very steep, slippery, sandy slope. Below us emerged the patchwork quilt of the fields of Dhe, stretching to the edge of the river bank. On the opposite bank was the village of Surkhang, only accessible from Dhe when the river is low enough to walk across, as it sits where the Puyung Khola meets the Kali Gandaki, and there is no bridge between the two villages. A suspension bridges crosses the Kali Gandaki river upstream of the meeting point between the two streams. We had just arrived at the bottom, outside the village of Dhe, when to our amazement Abhinav appeared on the white horse, galloping it down the same track we'd just inched our way down. He grinned from ear to ear as he pulled the horse up sharply at the bottom. The poor creature panted heavily, eyes bulging. Pradeep turned and shook his head.

The ex-monk I spoke to in the cafe back in Lo Manthang told me that Dhe, like Samdzong up near the border, had been complaining of a lack of water and asking to be relocated. It looked green enough to us, and people were busy harvesting in the fields, too busy, Pradeep apologised, to make us anything other than noodle soup for lunch. He promised us a good meal in Yara that night to make up for it, but since every single lodge had almost identical menus we didn't feel confident.

Actually Dhe had already begun the process of relocation, and the struggles to implement the move are indicative of the difficulties faced by the people of Mustang posed by their physical environment and local politics. According to a study done by Swiss NGO "Kam for Sud", a new site had been found for Dhe, on a plateau called Thangchung, south of the current site and at the confluence of the Kali Gandaki, the Dhe

Khola, and the Tsarang Khola, (*khola* is river in Nepali). Thangchung is just below Tsarang, the second largest village in Upper Mustang, and therefore one with a higher population and a greater number of animals who need more grazing land than the relatively tiny village of Dhe, which consisted of just twenty-four households, a total population of 158 people. Dhe claimed ownership of Thangchung on the basis of generational use, but nothing existed on paper to support this. Tsarang claimed it belonged to them. A fight to the death over this was narrowly avoided before an agreement was reached whereby Dhe could use the land for grazing but Tsarang could collect the six or seven annual tractor loads of dung for fuel and fertiliser. Then there were the physical difficulties of getting the water from the river to the plateau for grazing and drinking. Pumps couldn't be used because of the lack of electricity, and the river water was unsuitable for drinking. A spring existed just below Tsarang that could supply drinking water, but given that no love was lost between the two villages, Tsarang was unlikely to let Dhe use it. Some people outside of Dhe believe the village's troubles were caused by the selling of saligrams, others because they killed and skinned a yeti.

But as we sat in the warm dining room waiting for our noodle soup, we were oblivious to all of this. The room was much like all the dining rooms, with its mud benches covered in carpets running around the perimeter behind low, ornately painted tables. The walls were a blue-green and covered in the same pictures as in the other lodges: the panorama of Lhasa, a large painting of the Potala palace (the former residence of the Dalai Lama in Lhasa), photos of the Dalai Lama and Sakya Trinzen, some family photos, and a large silk thangka. Wires were strung loosely around the tops of the walls and ran down to two car batteries. One appeared to be for lighting, the other to power a small television inside a glass-fronted cabinet. The floor was hard and polished and the roof was held up by four tree trunk posts, painted maroon. The ceiling was covered, as was often the case, with pieces of fabric nailed to the beams.

Kitchen noises could be heard from behind the piece of fabric hanging in the doorway. Otherwise the place seemed deserted. While we waited, Abhinav was put to work carrying lunch out to the workers in the field, baskets of food and a thermos of tea. Dipak came in and gave us an apple each; here as in most of the villages there were plenty of apples.

Lunch over, Abhinav took the horses down and across the river, while the rest of us walked across the long metal suspension bridge. Below us, a thin milky blue stream ran. Clumps of poplars huddled close to the water's edge. Upstream, where the gorge narrowed, stood a small red chorten, its edges crumbling, towered over by the weathered cliffs, with horizontal layers of red, yellow, grey, and brown. The chorten looked forlorn. Did the spirits these were supposed to provide protection from feel diminished? Forgotten? Irrelevant? Would they take revenge? Perhaps this was the cause of Dhe's water problems. Or was it representative of the outward look that was loosening the connection to the natural world, the same disconnection occurring in the developed or minority world that has led us to over-consume and cause the world to overheat? Maybe we are the Hungry Ghosts, constantly craving but never satisfied.

CHAPTER 20

Yara

There was only one lodge open in Yara that night and it was full, so Pradeep and Dipak had to share a tent, which they pitched in a walled yard just above the lodge. Abhinav bedded down with the other porters on a bench in the dining room once all the tourists had gone to bed, which, I realised, was what he did every night. Still suffering somewhat from my cold, and struggling to fill my lungs with the thin air, I took to my bed for a while, while Neville went out to explore the village. For a long time I sat watching out the window next to my bed, as the light slowly faded. The small brown sparrows hopped about amongst the wood piles along the roof edges. Opposite, a barren hill rose, dotted with clumps of spiky bushes.

As I watched, three young men came sprinting and laughing down the steep track that ran along the base of the hill below a solitary house. Below us was the walled dirt yard by which we had entered, the horses laboriously pulling themselves up the several steps. Now as I watched, several men came galloping effortlessly up the steps on horses, pulling them up sharply in the yard where they quickly dismounted. Pradeep told us later that they were here on a pilgrimage to take their horses to bathe in the holy lake, Damodar Kunda. I noted that none of them wore a helmet.

When we arrived at the lodge, a little boy of about four greeted us cheekily in the entrance yard with "Pooh." In fact he greeted all foreigners with this. Now he, another boy of about the same age, and an older girl of about 11, had found their way to my window and stood there grinning and staring at me. The girl's behaviour wasn't much different from the younger children. We saw no other children of her age and I wondered whether, if there were others, they had been sent away to boarding school, as is common in Mustang, and she was destined to spend her life in the village because of some intellectual disability. I thought of the children at the disability centre. I knew those were the lucky few who received some intervention and therapy, albeit limited; the opportunities for a child like this in Upper Mustang would be zero. Disabled children in Nepal are often hidden away, seen as bringing shame on the family because it is believed they are being punished for their deeds in a previous incarnation.

Michel Peissel was told he was "sick in the head" by a porter whom he had acquired in Tsarang, and who helped him and his assistant Calay as they stumbled from Tsarang to Tangye and from Tangye finally to Yara, approaching it from the south while we came by the north-west. At the time of year that Peissel was travelling it was spring, the rivers were running high and he frequently found himself either having to wade through dangerous torrents or making detours over high passes, all on nothing but Tsampa, the traditional food eaten by the Loba. Tsampa is roasted and ground barley often mixed with salty Tibetan tea. Peissel had only peanut butter to mix with his on this particular part of the journey. He was determined, as was I, to see the remote Luri Gompa, but fortunately I had a warm comfortable bed—with ensuite—and a trekking menu, which was at least better than being forced to eat tsampa and peanut butter.

And we were right to not have too much faith in Pradeep's promise of a "good meal" that night to make up for noodle soup at lunch. By now we were fantasising about lamb cutlets, fresh vegetables, and a nice glass of wine. I dreamed of kissing the chef back in Pokhara when we returned, but for now, we had to choose as best we could which carb to go with tomato and cheese, and whether we wanted some powdered soup to start. It was our hot (powdered) lemon with a splash or three of "colour" that got us through now and that night we sat in a corner of the cosy dining room, drinking and snacking on the salty nuts and seeds that Dipak poured out for us. A group of French trekkers were there too, and unlike the many other French groups we came across, these ones were friendly. I was even able to resurrect my university French to converse, albeit awkwardly, with them, only to embarrass myself the next morning when one of them asked me:

"Ça va?" to which I of course replied,
"Oui ça va." and then to
"Et ta bon ami?",
"Oui merci."

For the rest of the day I was constructing a more correct answer in my head:

"Il est dans la chambre." "Il est en bon form, merci." "Il est putting on the same disgusting, sweaty trekking clothes he's been wearing for eight days now."

Neville's trekking clothes, after eight days, had taken on such a pungent aroma that it was all I could do not to dry retch as he pulled them on and off. I didn't sweat like him, especially since I wasn't exerting myself too much sitting on a horse.

That first night I was when I was woken by the ferocious barking of the great Tibetan mastiff chained up outside our door. For the first time

I felt in fear of my life from a wild animal; for the first time I was reduced from being a person to being prey. It tore away some of the insulation that keeps us all distanced from the "real" world, stripping me to my essential being. And for the first time I experienced true gratitude for the most basic of human needs: shelter.

But really I was basking in the self-indulgent privilege of flirting, albeit mildly, with death. In mere hours I could be plucked from the plateau by a helicopter and taken to a western-level hospital in Kathmandu. Meanwhile, Pradeep and Dipak were sleeping in a tent outside. Why was our safety more important than theirs?

I sat for a long time at the window looking up at the hill, lit up like day by the full moon, hoping I might see the elusive snow leopard, but nothing moved. The next morning I told Pradeep I'd been woken in the night.

"Yes, I hear jackals last night. First far away, then close to our tent," and his eyes widened.

"Jackals?" I replied. "Like a wild dog?"

"Mmm, no maybe more like a fox. In my village also. They eat chickens, maybe small goat."

So it probably wasn't even a snow leopard, just a pack of Himalayan jackals raising the hackles of all the village dogs. Evidence of brown bears has also been found in Upper Mustang. They live on small mammals, mostly marmots, and birds, but herders have reported losing yak calves, some horses and mules to bears. They aren't often seen, but bear scat has been found around Lo Manthang, in the Chhosar region, and near other villages, and they have been spotted in the Damodar Kunda region to the east of Yara. They tend not to come too close to villages although some researchers believe livestock reportedly taken by snow leopards may in fact have been taken by bears, judging from the hair samples left behind.^ Himalayan wolves also roam the Upper Mustang region and, like the snow leopard, have been killed by herders for taking livestock.*

So in theory, I could have been eaten by a few different carnivores, but even if I had actually been outside waiting for them, the fact that humans are a greater threat to them than they are to us makes my fantasy about being in danger just a little bit lame.

---

*https://www.researchgate.net/publication/301564266_Ancient_Himalayan_wolf_Canis_lupus_chanco_lineage_in_Upper_Mustang_of_the_Annapurna_Conservation_Area_Nepal_Launched_to_accelerate_biodiversity_research_A_peer-reviewed_open-access_journal]

*https://www.bearbiology.org/publications/ursus-archive/distribution-and-diet-of-brown-bears-in-the-upper-mustang-region-nepal/

CHAPTER 21

A Flying Monk and a Dangerous Goddess

We were about fifteen minutes into our trek to Luri Gompa when I realised I had left the pouch I always carried with my passport and phone, back at the lodge, where we were staying a second night after Luri. I needed the phone for photos and I never liked to be without my passport, no matter where I was. So Dipak, generous and tireless soul that he was, went back to get it for me.

Pradeep called, "Bistera, bistera," to Abhinav as we continued on—"slowly, slowly,"—to give Dipak time to catch up, but we'd been travelling for about half an hour and he still hadn't appeared.

"Rose, you are sure it is in your room?" asked Pradeep.

"Yes. It'll be on my bed."

"Ok."

And we ambled on. I got off the horse, because my knees were killing me, and walked for a while. We were travelling upstream along the northern bank of the Puyung Khola which joins the Kali Gandaki at Dhe and Surkhang. It was just a thin trickle in most places. There were caves high up in the cliffs, as well as at ground level with dry stone walled enclosures built around their openings. There were also some freestanding enclosures with very basic, rough shelters attached, which I imagine were for goats or sheep and their shepherds to take shelter.

We reached Luri and still no Dipak, but neither had the guy with the key arrived. Pradeep found he had phone coverage over on the rise above the river so walked over to call him. Meanwhile, Abhinav mounted the brown horse, bareback (it was carrying no packs because we were returning to Yara for another night), and took off to find Dipak. He found him waiting at the small village of Ghara. Dipak had taken the high road and, not being able to find us, had decided to wait there. And he had my pouch. Having found Dipak, Abhinav turned and rode back to Luri, while Dipak walked, arriving at the same time as the key holder. Pradeep, Neville and I were sitting on the ground waiting when Abhinav came galloping at full tilt. He pulled the horse up sharply and, with no saddle to hold him, pitched head first over the horse's head and onto the hard, rocky ground. We rushed over to see if he was ok, but he promptly picked himself up, tossed his head and said he was fine. He spent the next two days limping.

While Abhinav slept on the ground by the horses, the man with the key took us first to a small gompa on the flat ground high above the river. Strings of ragged prayer flags criss-crossed above it and fluttered in the breeze. Pradeep told us this gompa was only about one hundred years old. There were rooms attached to the main red-painted gompa, and a separate building next to it. It's possible that these were once inhabited by monks, but now no one lives at Luri. The guide unlocked the door and we entered a dimly lit room. It was like the other monasteries we'd visited but clearly little used. The guide lit a butter lamp and quietly intoned some prayers. Pradeep told us that someone comes early every morning to do this, or if there are visitors, will wait and do it then. After a quick look inside we followed the man out and waited while he lit a small fire of juniper in the courtyard and continued murmuring prayers.

Across the river the high red cliffs had been eroded into sharp pointed flutes, the eroded earth piled against the base and falling away into the narrow gorge. They resembled giant termite mounds. Caves dotted the lower parts.

"Ah!" cried Pradeep, pointing at a very sharp, high flute. "I see this when I come here last time, but I thought in the earthquake maybe it has fall down, but still there."

The flute had a flat disk-shape that appeared to balance on top. It protruded high above the rest of the cliff. The guide looked up as well and then spoke to Pradeep, explaining something. Pradeep translated: "He says there was very powerful lama living in a cave here," he said, and turned to point at the caves in the cliffs behind us. "Every morning, he is fly across the river, and build this, err, stone here on top."

I pictured the lama calmly leaving his spartan cave each morning and flying across in the thin, cold air, his maroon robes flapping, to place another piece on the point he was building. There was a stone wall enclosure that had been built out from the base of the cliff on our side of the gorge, which Pradeep said had been used for monks who wished to meditate for long periods. People from the nearby village would bring food each day. The walls were now crumbling, the stones falling away down the slope.

"The monks looking for the quiet place with nobody disturbing. And these monks are powerful," said Pradeep with awe.

Stories of monks undertaking seemingly impossible feats abound in Tibetan lore. It is said that having learned and meditated upon the nature of reality they can manipulate it. Scientific studies have proven Tummo, the conscious ability to increase body temperature, to be true. Despite freezing temperatures and even in snow, monks, by employing this breathing technique, can increase their body temperature by almost ten degrees celsius. It is rumoured this is how Alexandra David-Neel managed to survive the cold during her journey through Tibet.

Explorer and travel writer M. G. Hawking claims to have discovered a village tucked away in a Himalayan valley where he met people who could perform extraordinary feats, one being the very useful ability to refill his cup of chang as long as he left some in the bottom. He saw a dead bird brought back to life and a sleeping person made to get up and walk into another room without waking, all through the use of mind powers learned through study and meditation. Hawking claims that if one understands quantum physics and therefore that what we understand as reality is in fact an illusion then these things are perfectly plausible.

In Tibet I asked Tenzin if he thought it possible that monks could fly and manifest things. He believed they could but they are not supposed to as it would take their focus away from their main purpose, to free themselves of all worldly attachment. If a monk were to focus on manifesting material things this could lead to greed, one of the three human failings that will send you down the bad karmic path of rebirth into one of the undesirable realms. Tenzin did however tell me of an incident he remembered from his childhood.

"Once, when we were on holiday, my father was driving along and saw a nun walking along the road. He stopped and offered her a lift, but she refused, saying she would rather walk."

So they continued on to the next village, but when they arrived the nun was already there.

We began the climb to the cave gompa. We passed three crumbling chortens with poles stuck in their tops and prayer flags strung between them. Little remained of the paint and engravings on the sides. One had completely collapsed and was just a mound of yellow clay with some stones sticking out. A square red building sat perched high up on the cliff but the gompa itself was inside one of the caves. To reach this we had to follow a steep track up and across a metal bridge, covered along its length with prayer flags, and then up higher still until we reached a cave below the building. We entered and climbed a wooden ladder. Beside the new ladder sat the old one, a notched log such as we had seen in Lo Manthang and other villages. We huffed and puffed in the thin air. Dipak joked: "Mt Everest!"

We entered a small cave where there were several smallish statues set against the back wall. Behind these were silk thangkas. In front was an old cabinet along which were some small bowls, and beside this a low table with a couple of butter lamps on it. On the left was a small chorten. Large tea pots and other vessels sat on other tables and on the uneven floor. Everything was grimy with dirt and soot. The guide lit the lamps and stood chanting prayers in a low voice while we waited quietly. He then unlocked a door on the left and we entered a small cave that was almost entirely filled with a polished, ornately painted chorten. Pradeep pointed to the outer wall where there was a section made from mud.

"This was open, but now block," he said, "because people is coming to take things. Maybe Khampas. This area many Khampas. Maybe Khampas destroy and find the gold or something."

"Gold?" I asked.

"Inside the chorten they put in there normally gold or many valuable things. And mantra also."

Of all the chortens and paintings we had seen in the monasteries we'd visited, this one was unique. It is known as the "Hundred Thousand Dragons Chorten". Luri belongs to a sub-sect of the Kagyu school of Buddhism, a sect which came after the Nyingmapa and Sakya sects of Lo Gekar and the monasteries of Lo Manthang and was established in about the twelfth century. The Kagyu sect has a heavy emphasis on tantric meditation, believing that enlightenment can be reached in one lifetime if meditation is practiced enough, which I guess explains the meditation cell and the possibility of powerful flying lamas. Nobody knows who built Luri Gompa but it is estimated to have been built in the thirteenth or fourteenth century. The paintings on the highly polished chorten and on the domed ceiling and walls around it resembled the art of central Asian countries and was quite different to the monasteries of Lo Manthang and throughout Mustang. Images of high lamas were painted on the domed ceiling above, and below these were white flowers, something like chrysanthemums, on curling stems and with white leaves on a green background. At the very top of the ceiling above the chorten was an intricate mandala. The chorten itself looked and felt more like enamel than the clay from which it was built, so smooth and polished was its surface.

Along the inside wall something had been painted in large Tibetan script.

"Is this 'om mane padme hum'? I asked Pradeep.

He consulted with the guide who read the script quietly muttering some 'oms' and 'padmes' under his breath. He then explained to Pradeep who translated: "Is different mantra. 'Om mane padme hum' *normalment* but little bit mixed."

Next to the door a sequence of vertical lines had been painted, like someone keeping tally and the guide said he thought it may have been someone keeping count of the circumambulations of the chorten, but he really didn't know.

Stooping through the low doorway again, we returned to the room with the statues. Opposite was another small wooden door.

"What's in there Pradeep?" I asked. He spoke to the guide then turned to me.

"This is a little dangerous," he explained in a low, serious voice. "When it is the ceremony time they open, but is…like the goddess."

"It's dangerous for us because the goddess doesn't like to be disturbed?"

"Yes."

We climbed another ladder and emerged onto the roof of the red building to find a small solar panel. From here we looked down through a hole into an adjoining cave where the guide had again lit a fire in a small hearth in the middle of the room and was intoning more prayers. There was a shallow depression in the inner wall that looked like a small fireplace but with no chimney, which would explain the blackened walls and ceiling. Above it a ledge had been cut like a mantlepiece, and on this sat some rocks and a tarnished vessel with a very narrow neck. A copper bowl sat on a battered, broken, wooden, table, which had a thick coating of dust. More caves could be seen through holes in this cave. The cliff was honeycombed with caves.

"I think so, many house before; many room, many house," said Pradeep.

He was guessing. Not much is known about any of Mustang's caves. They're estimated to be around 3000 years old and it's assumed people lived in them at some time. Maybe Luri's caves were inhabited by a community of monks, maybe the monks took them over after they had been long abandoned. I like the fact that the caves, the monastery, the extraordinary chorten and the unusual paintings are still a mystery.

We joined Abhinav, lying on the rocky ground enjoying his sleep, and ate some of Dipak's dried fruit and nuts and I pulled out the apple I'd save from Dhe. I ate half and gave the rest to the white horse. There was not another soul around. The guide had locked up and gone back to his village. We sat and relaxed in the sun. Across the gorge, the sharp fluted peaks that formed the cliff were topped with a completely flat, plain. The barren hills rose beyond them rolling away to the south in yellow-brown waves, and far away on the horizon, peaks topped with patches of snow.

Our small picnic finished, Abhinav re-saddled my horse and we set off for the village of Ghara. We passed ancient ruins, solitary walls of mud with small window holes and jagged tops, their edges softened by centuries of weather. Some still vaguely framed long-abandoned dwellings and low dry stone walls fenced in imaginary people and animals. A small chorten stood by the path, a hole in one side and wooden sticks poking out the top, but with no prayer flags.

Abhinav riding the brown horse became impatient with our slow pace and kept spurring his horse to go faster, which then made my horse speed up. No amount of pulling on the reins to slow it down or kicking it to make it go faster worked if the other horse was setting the pace. We quickly broke into a trot and before I knew it, for the first time I was cantering. For a second I thought I was going to fall off, but I heard my riding teacher's voice saying "Legs on!" and gripped tight with my legs, and "Core on!" and tightened my stomach muscles and thus managed to stay on until we reached a solitary, low house well ahead of the others. I let out a sound of exasperation and Abhinav looked around at me with a grin. We dismounted and, after tethering the horses to a couple of bushes where some washing had been draped to dry, he left me and went into the house.

I had decided to sit down and write a few notes while I waited for the others to catch up, when I heard a call behind me and turned to see an old woman with long, wet, grey hair. She beckoned me to come in. As I approached the door, she picked up a round metal tray full of noodles that had been drying in the sun. She led me into a courtyard where a man was sitting on the ground grinding some yellow grain against a flat hand-mill. The woman put the tray on the ground and motioned for me to enter the kitchen and sit down. All we could do was smile and nod at each other but I was touched by her hospitality. I sat on a seat by the window and looked at her stove. It sat in the middle of the light, sunny, room and was a small, black stove with room for two pots and a chimney going up through the ceiling. On the short end opposite the chimney was a receptacle into which fuel went and next to this was a cut-down plastic container filled with sheep or goat dung pellets and a scoop. The woman stood combing out her long, wet, hair still smiling at me. A couple of shelves set into the wall held cooking implements and in a glass cabinet were bottles of beer, spirits and plastic bottles of water, so it looked like they took in tourists when there were any. The place was so remote I wondered how often they got any business.

I assumed this was where we were having lunch, but suddenly Abhinav appeared at the door saying, "Ok." The others had finally caught up and we set off again. Once again Abhinav took me on a terrifying joyride, geeing the horses into a trot and then a canter. Thankfully we soon arrived at Ghara, which as far as I could tell had only two buildings, one being the tea house. They can't have been prepared for guests because

Pradeep had brought our usual picnic of yak cheese and tinned sardines but he had the owner make us fresh Tibetan bread. She also served us some sausages, like hotdogs, which after our bland trekking diet, tasted great. We washed it all down with hot milk tea.

As usual, Pradeep and Dipak sat in the kitchen chatting with the owner while we sat alone in the dining room as the guests. After a while we could hear yelling and a thumping noise. At first we thought it was Abhinav harassing the horses, but went out to find two men sitting on sheep skins with a rug on the ground between them playing a game with shells and coins, with Abhinav and a couple of other men keenly watching. This was a game called "Sho", a Tibetan gambling game. Each player yelled out a number as two dice were shaken in a cup and then slammed down hard on several layers of leather. They then shuffled the shells between them and threw the dice again. In Tibet we witnessed many men playing this game and Tenzin even taught Neville to play using an app. It is played in a similar way to backgammon.

We returned to the dining room and waited for Pradeep to finish chatting in the kitchen. He eventually appeared with the owner of the lodge, a woman who looked to be in her thirties who smiled broadly at us, then promptly held up a mobile phone and took a photo of Neville and I.

"Her daughter is working in Cyprus," Pradeep told us proudly.

The contrast between that Mediterranean island and this tiny, remote village perched on a high, barren desert was stark. We thanked her for her hospitality and set off for the short journey back to Yara.

And again I was at the mercy of the impatient and mischievous Abhinav, but at one point Dipak ran up and took hold of my horse because the boy was about to lead me galloping down a steep slippery gravel path and by then they all knew I was no horse-woman. I stayed on the horse, but Dipak led it carefully down the path until it was safe for me to take the reins again only to have Abhinav whip his horse up again and we both came tearing into Yara at top speed and up the steps to the lower terrace of our lodge, narrowly avoiding the two small boys who were playing there. I jumped down and shook my head at him and he grinned from ear to ear.

That evening, as we sat drinking in the dining room before dinner, a young woman came in to tell us that there would be Tibetan dancing and singing after dinner. I thought we might be joining in with the dancers and singers, but we sat around the perimeter of the small courtyard and half a dozen women gathered in a line and began, quite self-consciously at first, to sing for us. They sang in nasal voices, swinging their legs in synchronised fashion, arms around shoulders, laughing at themselves when they briefly forgot how the song went, joining in with gusto when someone recovered the faltering song and it got going again. Between songs they would discuss amongst themselves what they should sing next, but we were never told what any of them meant.

Some of the men, who had been drinking raksi for a couple of hours by the time the singing began, joined in at certain points, yelling drunkenly and clapping enthusiastically and seeming to call out requests. After about half an hour a bowl was produced and we were asked to make a "donation". I threw 500 rupees into the bowl and we went to bed, as did most of the foreign guests. The locals carried on for some time after. Having lost all track of days of the week, I realised it was Saturday night—a wild Saturday night in Yara, high up on the Tibetan plateau far from everywhere. I guess this is how most of the world amused themselves before reliable electricity enabled TV, radio, recorded music, and computers to stop us from singing and dancing together.

CHAPTER 22

Tsarang

As we set out for Tsarang, first we followed the rough road high above the river. Opposite were the fluted cliffs honeycombed with caves and at the top, completely flat, dark, grey plains. It was impossibly dry and barren. Even the stunted bushes grew sparse on the yellow hilly desert spread before and behind us. Then Neville, Pradeep, and Dipak took a narrow track, leaving me at the mercy of Abhinav with whom I descended to the river bed and criss-crossed the river back towards Dhe. He whooped and yelled loudly to hear his voice echo off the cliffs and called especially loudly when we saw people out harvesting in the fields, making them look up from their work.

Since the brown horse carried our packs, Abhinav wasn't riding and couldn't gee my horse up, but at some point we became separated and I found myself alone on a horse determined to get to Dhe. I had no idea whether Pradeep intended for us to head through Dhe, but I just had to let the horse go and it climbed up the river bank and into the village, ambling along the paths between houses and by the stone-walled fields and groves of trees, passing a wall of prayer wheels on the left as though it knew the protocol. The place was deserted but for an old woman and a little girl washing clothes at a tap. The old woman replied to my "Namaste" with little enthusiasm and the little girl stared up at me with a serious face.

I realised the horse knew exactly where it was going when it suddenly stopped at the doorway of a walled yard, turned and entered. As my head hit the top of the doorway I finally had cause to be thankful for the wretched helmet. I don't know whether the horse had smelled it or made a note of it on our previous visit, but it must have felt very pleased with itself because the yard was filled with cut grass spread out and drying in the sun. But before it could set about eating the village's precious store of winter feed, I dismounted and managed to turn the creature and pull it out of the yard. I was terrified someone was going to see me and think I was stealing their hay. Abhinav eventually turned up and we sat and waited in silence for the others. As it happened we did need to stop in Dhe so we could be registered at the check-post. This was the first time I became aware this was necessary. All foreign trekkers had to be registered at checkpoints throughout Upper Mustang.

Pradeep decided they would once again take the narrow track along the cliff while we would travel along the river bed, so we doubled back while they went on and travelled along, criss-crossing the rivulets once again, with Abhinav continuing to whoop and call.

It was easy to see how the area had once been an ocean. In places the water ran clear blue over white sand. I wished we could have stopped and waded in the water, even though it was freezing. In that bright sunshine it would have felt like being by an ocean inlet and I wanted to see what was in the wide deep pools. To my delight I found a piece of a saligram at the edge of one streamlet. It was peaceful travelling along that wide river bed with huge cliffs towering either side, but as the morning wore on our old friend the wind came up. But before it became too ferocious, we rejoined the others and rounded a point before heading up the Tsarang Khola. We passed a large stone dwelling standing alone on the edge of the river bed, crossed a wooden bridge and began ascending a track that climbed along the side of the cliff. Three people came walking towards us with horses laden with packs, exchanged a few words with Pradeep and Dipak as they passed, and strode energetically away from us. As the track went on it became stonier—large slippery stones that clinked under the horses' hooves—but then we turned and began to climb a very steep slope, straight up the cliff, covered with the same large stones. It was very hard going. The horses eyes bulged and they breathed heavily and frequently slipped and threatened to lose their footing. I think they were scared; I certainly felt more afraid for them than for myself. When we finally reached the top I dismounted and hobbled to a ledge to sit down and rub my aching knees.

Dipak who still hardly seemed out of breath after the steep climb, came over and sympathetically rubbed my knee as well.

"Very steep," I said to him.

"Yes," he replied, "very dangerous."

We sat and waited while Pradeep and finally Neville came toiling up. The horses wandered, grazing on tufts of green grass fed by a narrow stream that meandered along before falling to the khola we'd left behind. Depressingly, I noted the rubbish that lay in the shallow water—bits of plastic packaging. We were now on the outskirts of Tsarang, Mustang's largest village after Lo Manthang.

When Pradeep and Neville arrived, we waited while everyone recovered before continuing on into the village. We travelled along a pathway between stone walls enclosing groves of poplar trees. Some horses were penned in one walled yard and in a field also surrounded by a low stone wall a man was working with two strange looking beasts, like black and white cows but with large yak horns.

"Yaks?" I asked Dipak.

"Dzos," he replied.

Dzos are a cross between cows and yaks. The females, actually called Dzomos, are fertile while the males, Dzos, are sterile. Yaks are rare in Upper Mustang now. In 1988 Nepal and China agreed to stop all animal migration across the border, which meant that the people of Upper Mustang could no longer take their animals up to the high pastures to graze as they had traditionally done. Goats and sheep can be taken down to lower altitudes to feed in the winter, but yaks can't survive at lower altitudes.

Pradeep led us through Tsarang and almost out the other side before stopping at the Kailash Guest House. While he went in to see to about our accommodation, Neville and I sat outside on a ledge in the sun and waited. A short wizened woman with knobbly hands saw us and, smiling broadly with a mouthful of ancient teeth, and speaking in a high, nasal voice, beckoned enthusiastically for us to enter. We emerged into the brightly lit inner courtyard and could hear a lone female voice chanting and the ringing of small cymbals coming from somewhere. The whole place was bustling with people coming and going. Pradeep saw us and took us upstairs to our room. The room and the ensuite were lit by two skylights and a window looked out onto a tree garden. There was no hot water, but I was stupidly desperate to wash my hair and succeeded in giving myself a headache after washing it in the ice-cold water over the sink. I lay shivering in my bed afterwards trying to get warm.

A photo of Tsarang is on the front cover of my copy of Peissel's book. When I showed it to Pradeep he said, "I think you will see more trees now." He was right. The village in Peissel's picture shows bright green, walled fields but few trees, but now trees grow all through and around the village. Two buildings dominate Tsarang: the monastery and the huge, five-storey, palace.

Michel Peissel spent a lot of time in Tsarang where he stayed in the monastery at the invitation of the abbott. The abbott was the son of the Raja of Lo. He left his monastery to marry and had a son. His wife died when the boy was only four-years-old so the monk decided to return to his monastic way of life, confining himself within the royal apartments of the Tsarang monastery.

The son was living there with him and about a dozen elderly monks when Peissel came to stay. That boy is now the Crown Prince of Lo, or *Gyalchung*, the boy whom the King and Queen adopted.

The monastery at Tsarang is very large. The entry to the main hall was covered by a black woollen fabric, but it was barely a covering, with large holes torn in it. Some of the smaller holes had been stitched closed with thick white thread. Peissel describes "a gigantic brown yak-wool veil" covering the entrance when he went there. That one had two Buddhist symbols that look like reverse Swastikas, one on each side. The position of the two largest holes in the current piece correspond to the positions of the symbols on the one Peissel saw and I couldn't help but wonder whether this was the same piece of material and someone had deliberately torn them out.

Inside the main hall, ornately carved wooden and glass cabinets, beautifully painted with gold and other colours, housed the many Buddha statues.

"In thirteenth century this monastery is built," Pradeep said.

"But this carving is beautiful. Is it new?" I asked

"Yes. This the new one. I was here maybe 1992 I think so and it not here like that."

There was a carving of a deer and a peacock riding dragons. Unlike the pair of golden deer seen atop many Tibetan monasteries, including the one at Tsarang, a single deer represents harmony, happiness, faithfulness, peace and longevity, their serene natures seen as infinitely compassionate. The peacock represents romantic love and beauty. It is able to kill snakes with its talons and has the ability to change poison into nectar. The dragon represents the strong male yang energy and is a creature of great creative power.

There was certainly plenty of destructive energy going on outside the monastery. Now that we were back by the Kali Gandaki gorge we were once again being whipped by the wind and we could hear doors banging relentlessly in the gale.

The usual 108 books were also housed in the cabinets but over by a side wall an enormous number of books had been stacked; Pradeep guessed there were more than 1000. They had, until recently, been kept in the ancient crumbling palace but, because of water damage after the recent earthquake, they were moved to the monastery for safe keeping. The whole place looked to be in far better condition than any of the other monasteries we visited. There was even a microphone by the abbot's seat and a speaker. However, like most of the others, it had not escaped the earthquake unscathed and a large crack ran down one wall. Pradeep told us there were forty-two monks currently attached to the monastery, a lot more than when Peissel visited, but a far cry from the 2000 that it had once housed.

Pradeep pointed to one picture of the Buddha sitting in the most familiar position with one hand laid in his lap while the other points towards the earth. He then tried to explain something to me:

"This kind of position, when the Buddha come…" he paused, clicking his tongue in frustration saying, "I forget what this is calling. Mmm, when they have to, when they get all things…mmm they touch the…. somebody, err." He stopped then said, "You see those two deer over there, that also the same history, so when is in light, err…"

"When he reaches enlightenment?" I offered

"Yes that time only the deer is see to Buddha."

"When he reaches enlightenment, only then he can see the deer?"

"Yes."

It was often frustrating for both of us when Pradeep knew so much, but couldn't convey it in English and it made me wish I spoke more Nepali than "go upstairs".

"Rose," Pradeep then called me over to the altar, and Neville and I went over to light lamps once again. "Last monastery," he said with a giggle.

We lit a butter lamp each then left to explore the old palace accompanied by one of the monks as guide. He wore a t-shirt over his maroon robes, Nike trainers on his feet, and a rust coloured jacket, while pushed up onto his shaved head were a pair of sporty, fluorescent-armed sunglasses.

On our first trip to Nepal, Neville took the boys (for some respite) to the cinema in Kathmandu where they were showing one of the Narnia movies. Sitting in the row in front of them were some monks in maroon robes. At the interval (when an attendant came to take their orders for refreshments) they watched as the monks took out mobiles phones and sat dabbing busily at the screens. At dinner that evening they told our host parents, about the monks and their phones.

"Tibetan monks," they said, and exchanged a knowing look of disdain.

The monastery sat on a ridge high above the river and the palace a little higher along the same ridge. The wind hammered us as we walked. One side of the palace looked like a fort, the top crumbling away like so many of the ruins we had seen further north. The other part looked more intact and some of the windows on the side facing the monastery had been replaced, although one was completely bricked up.

We climbed rough stone stairs and the monk unlocked a wooden door. It had been one hundred years or more since the King of Lo used this palace as a residence and it was all but a ruin. Still, the chapel had lamps lit and the seven bowls of water set before its golden gods each morning. I marvelled that it hadn't fallen down in the earthquake and prayed there would be no tremors as we clambered up a rickety ladder and onto an internal balcony which railings were long gone. The whole place was dirt, dust, and crumbling stone walls and timbers. One room appeared to have been the "bathroom", two timber-framed holes in the floor falling the three storeys to the ground below—the traditional style toilet still used by Loba and which Manjushree Thapa found in the palace in Lo Manthang. I followed Pradeep into an adjoining room but he quickly turned and ushered me out saying,

"Is dirty."

It stunk, and not of animal dung.

The guide then unlocked a door into what was another small chapel but was filled with ancient, mediaeval-looking weapons all hanging on the wall or sitting on dusty shelves as though they'd sat there since being put away after the last battle. In 1964 Michel Peissel visited the same room and, from the way he described it, nothing about it had changed. To my amazement even the most gruesome object was still there. Hanging on a hook alongside some of the other implements was a black, shrivelled human hand, its nails curved, hard and smooth. Peissel was told that it was the hand of a thief which had been cut off as punishment, but when Pradeep asked the monk he had a different story.

"One who is building this…working," began Pradeep, "then…same king is thinking—this very bad thinking—same palace not other place…build. For that they cut so after he is not going to work other."

"Oh, they cut off the builder's hand so he couldn't go away and build another palace for someone else?"

"Yes!"

"It must be very old," I said.

"Yes. Not less than…more than two centuries old."

Very bad thinking indeed.

Neville had found a box covered in skulls and asked Pradeep what was in it. Pradeep asked the monk.

"Somethings very dead," said Pradeep, and laughed.

Hanging on the wall above was a suit of chainmail and I lifted part of it. It was very heavy.

"Is iron, I think so," said Pradeep.

Next to it was a helmet and then what looked like a breast plate made of some kind of thin bone.

"Yes I think so one animal," Pradeep tried to explain. "What calling maybe this area I don't think so. This found…lower place."

"Is it shell?" I asked

"This, you know is skin. Is out of skin this kind of things."

"Like a crocodile?"

"Mmm, not crocodile. Other is, this kind is very similar. Is walking like the crocodile in the forest. In some place they find now also. From our village also they found also, mm, like a lizard."

"Like a big lizard?"

"Like the…I don't know so English name."

I really had no idea. Nepal has a creature called a gharial that lives in the jungle rivers. It is just like a crocodile, but has a long, very narrow snout with a bulbous growth on the end. Maybe it was a gharial skin.

The monk told us it was too dangerous to visit the rest of the palace and anyway, Pradeep explained, there was not much else to see, just a whole lot more empty, dusty, rooms, but we were allowed to climb up to the next floor from which we'd get a good view of the village as long as we didn't stay up there too long. We were now on the fourth floor and through frameless window holes we could see all of Tsarang spread out below us, its neat white-washed houses, their roofs lined with stacked timber, surrounded everywhere by green trees. We even looked down now on the monastery over on its high ridge. On the far side of the village was the large entrance chorten from the cover of Peissel's book and, beyond this, brown plains where the wind was whipping up the dust towards the dull hills beyond. Pradeep told us we would be heading that way the next day. He then pointed out a hole in the floor where the earth was crumbling away, and so we quickly climbed down and out.

CHAPTER 23

Life and Death

When we returned to the lodge, the chanting and cymbals had started again. A buddhist nun was sitting alone on a chair facing a blank wall, at the foot of which was some incense burning. She alternated chanting, clicking her fingers, and ringing small cymbals. Pradeep said a man from the family had died after an operation in Kathmandu about a month before and now the appropriate ceremonies were being conducted. This period after someone dies is called the *bardo*, the time between death and rebirth, and goes on for forty-nine days. The last ceremony is held in the monastery at which time the piece of paper, on which the name of the dead person given to him by a lama at his birth, is burnt, thus releasing his spirit.

That night at dinner were another large group of French. I greeted them as we entered the dining room, but got only a desultory response. Instead, I got chatting to a woman who was sitting on her own. She was from Germany and was trekking to Lo Manthang with her husband, a guide and a porter, but her husband had become very sick and was upstairs in bed. He had started vomiting way back in Pokhara, she presumed from food poisoning, but had not got any better, and now he was having trouble breathing in the thin air because he was an asthmatic.

Being an asthmatic myself, and not having that much trouble breathing, I thought this sounded odd.

"Have you tried him with some garlic soup?" I suggested.

"Oh, he can't keep anything down," she responded.

"It's bronchitis!" one of the French men suddenly blurted into the conversation. He was a doctor who had examined the man. Bronchitis, in my nursing and personal experience, did not generally include constant vomiting, but I was clearly out-ranked so kept my mouth shut.

"Anyway, I've asked him what he wants me to do with him if he dies," she said matter-of-factly. I stared in astonishment. "Well, I have to know what he wants. These things can happen." I marvelled at her cold, German pragmatism.

Later in our room, Neville, being a much more seasoned trekker than me and having been lectured more than once on the perils of ignoring the symptoms of altitude sickness, remarked to me that this could well be what was wrong with the man.

The next morning at six sharp I was almost catapulted out of my bed by the harsh blaring of trumpets and clashing cymbals.

"What the fuck?" I said. Neville laughed. "How long's that been going on?"

"Not much before you woke up," he replied.

The trumpets and clashing cymbals were followed by the drone of monks chanting, the tone alternating up and down. They were on the other side of the wall from me and the ceremony continued all morning without a break with the family going back and forth delivering food and tea to them.

As we were heading in to breakfast I saw the German woman.

"How is your husband?" I asked.

"Oh, he's much worse," she said, with little emotion. "He's delirious. He asks me something and I answer but five minutes later he asks the same question. So I've decided I'll leave him with the guide who can help him get dressed and they can travel up to Lo Manthang by jeep, and I'll continue on with the porter."

Life and Death

I was speechless. Vomiting and delirium are both symptoms of altitude sickness and the worst possible thing you can do with someone suffering from this is to take them to a higher altitude. But she said the French doctor had examined him, given him something, and deemed him fit to travel.

"Well, good luck," I said, but inside I was screaming, "You selfish cow! Your husband might have altitude sickness, this might kill him, but even if it isn't altitude sickness, how could you make him get up and dressed and undergo a rough jeep ride just so you can see Lo Manthang?!"

In 2019, on our trip through Tibet, I experienced serious altitude sickness at Everest Base Camp. The night before we had spent at 4300 metres in a dusty truck stop of a town called Shegar. I hadn't slept well and had a constant headache so I was a little worried about ascending another 700 metres. By the time we reached Base Camp all I wanted to do was lie down, so I did. I managed to rouse myself after some lunch and visit the Rongbuk monastery, but as soon as the tour was over I returned to the tent and lay down. Even as a headache grew and blossomed in the front of my skull, and even when I detected it was becoming a little harder to breathe, I kept assuring Neville and Tenzin if I rested I'd be ok. But Tenzin was worried.

"Rose," he said, "I think maybe we should go down. We have seen everything here and the buses stop running after 8pm. And altitude sickness usually gets worse at night."

Reluctantly, and with a few tears at my failure to sleep the night at Base Camp I agreed. Within an hour of descending 700 metres, I felt fine, but I often thought of that poor German man in Tsarang while I was feeling ill.

Three days after we left Tsarang, we watched a helicopter fly up the gorge and return about half an hour later. I couldn't help wondering if it was rescuing the German man or retrieving his body.

CHAPTER 24

Shyanmochen

The entrance chorten on Michel Peissel's book cover is worn and colourless compared with the beautifully restored version that we passed on our way out of Tsarang. The once dull engravings of elephants, horses, peacocks and a winged woman with the legs of a bird—one creature for each of four sides—are now vividly clear and beautifully pastel-coloured. The winged woman is the "kinnara" or "shang shang", a celestial musician who represents enlightenment. A creature from the Himalayas, she is said to watch over people in trouble or danger. The chorten was surrounded by barbed wire so we couldn't walk through it.

Once again, Abhinav was late with the horses, so Pradeep, Neville and I set out alone, but before we went over the rise I let them go on while I sat and waited. A shepherd came up the hill with his flock of goats, whistling to them as he went, taking them out to graze on the sparse foliage. His whistling and the tinkling of the goats' bells were the only sound; as they faded away there was complete silence. That was until, back down the hill towards Tsarang came the whistling and "ya! ya!" of Dipak trying to get the horses moving faster. The brown horse came toiling up the hill with our packs, and both it and the white horse looked fed up with the whole expedition.

We were now on the way down, but Pradeep took us via a slightly different route so that we weren't covering the same ground. We passed Tragmar in the distance, its high red cliffs unmissable and now passed the famous long mane wall, on its left side in keeping with Buddhist tradition, where the goddess' (or demon's depending on which version) intestines were enclosed after her defeat. This 240 metre long stone wall, which follows the contours of the land, stepping down in sections, is painted pale yellow at the top, with vertical stripes of yellow, grey and white along the bottom. On top are flat stones inscribed with "Om mane padme hum".

Following the path that led between the stone-walled fields just below the village of Ghemi, we were brought to a complete halt by a wall that blocked the path. Stones had been placed to enable climbing over, but this was no good for the horses. Pradeep, ever-patient, seemed genuinely annoyed at what seemed a deliberate attempt to force traffic back and through the village, presumably to improve business. But it was poor Abhinav who now had to double back and take the horses the long way round while we climbed over and continued along the path. And we were now, once again, heading for the Nyi La pass, our exit from the Kingdom of Lo and the highest point. While Neville and Pradeep powered on up the slope, I lagged behind with Dipak shepherding me until I was willing myself to just put one foot in front of the other, but it wasn't long before I had to admit defeat. I lack stamina at sea-level; at 3500 metres and after almost ten days on the move, I was seriously out of energy. Feeling like an utter failure, I sat down on a rock, with Dipak a short distance away, and had to wait once again for the horses. We sat in silence. We had little common language and there was nothing to say anyway.

After about twenty minutes Abhinav finally appeared, yelling at the horses as usual, whistling and throwing rocks. Earlier that day, he'd thrown a rock at the horses and it had bounced off the back of the brown horse and whistled past me millimetres from my face. Pradeep yelled sternly at him, the only time I ever heard him raise his voice. I turned to look at Abhinav and he gave me a sheepish grin.

Neville and I had been discussing how much in tips we should give to each of our "staff", agonising about it really, because there are no clear guidelines, but it's very poor form indeed to not tip your porters and guide. In the end, Neville asked Pradeep what he thought we should tip the other two and suggested 5000 Nepalese rupees for Abhinav (about A$70).

"Too much I think," Pradeep replied. "He's very lazy."

"4000?" Nev suggested.

"Mmm, yes maybe," he replied, but it seemed like he didn't think the boy deserved much at all. He had known Abhinav since he was a young boy.

"Now he is smoking and drinking raksi," he told us.

Abhinav and I reached the top of the Nyi La ahead of the others, with me riding and him holding the tail of the poor brown horse, and as we sat on the stones to wait for the others I said, "I could never have done this without the horses."

To which he replied, rolling his eyes and with a rare burst of fluent English: "We know!"

We left three mountain bikers (two trekkers and their guide) on the top of the pass trying to fix a broken wheel and descended to the tiny village of Jaite where we had lunch, with the added luxury of some tinned pineapple for desert. I asked to use the toilet and was directed to a key hanging on a post in the entry courtyard. This house, a lodge, was literally the only building for miles around and as I crossed the trail to the outhouse I wondered why the thing had to be kept locked. I suppose trekkers passing through might use it, but this might mean a handful of people a day during the high season. It's not as though there was even any toilet paper to steal.

As I returned the key to its hook, I noticed a rough wooden loom in a corner of the courtyard where a thin piece of the striped material seen on nearly all the women was being woven. Spools of brightly-coloured thread sat in a plastic container atop a gas canister next to the loom. I now saw that all the pieces of this fabric I had seen were made from three strips of this woven material sewn together.

About 4pm we wearily arrived at the "Hotel Nilgiri and Restaurant", one of three guest houses that make up the village of Shyanmochen. Just inside the front door, in a room to the left where the porters were gathered, a traditional stove roared ferociously. This guest house was a work in progress. Our room was in a newly added section at the front of the building, and plywood walls lined the passageway.

A large group of Swiss doctors commandeered the main dining room that night. They were camping in the yard next to the lodge and were travelling from village to village treating people. Seeing this room full, we sat and waited at the large dining table in another common area, but Pradeep appeared and ushered us instead through the kitchen to an adjoining room where, instead of being the isolated, honoured guests, we joined a middle-aged couple from Holland, their guide and porter, and a man and his son who were taking horses up to Tsarang next morning for a trekking group. We watched our hostess as she went about preparing food with Dipak helping. Pradeep encouraged us to add more and more "colour" to our hot lemon and we all shared stories in English and Nepali. We could understand enough words of Nepali to get the gist of what was being said. I felt like I was in Izaak Walton's *The Compleat Angler* (published in 1653), wandering the countryside and staying at the next inn. I'm pretty sure if we'd caught a fish during our travels, our hostess would have happily cooked it for us.

When she'd done cooking, our hostess sat on a low stool and joined in the conversation. Next to her was a cone-shaped mound of what looked like biscuit dough. It was a mound of tsampa and when I asked whether I could try some, she cheerfully handed it over. I broke off a lump and put it in my mouth. It tasted how it looked: like biscuit dough, slightly sweet and buttery, but coarser. Tsampa is still a staple of Tibetan diets.

Roasted barley is ground to a flour and often mixed with butter tea (tea with butter and salt). The guide and porter sitting opposite us had put some in their warm raksi, and it formed a sludge in the bottom of the glass. I guess it added some flavour to that otherwise vile liquid. There was also a jug of chhang, an alcoholic beverage usually made from fermented barley or rice. This was the first time I'd seen it, probably because it is usually only served to the porters and guides unless a trekker specifically asks for it, so I tried some of this too. It tasted like fruit juice left in the fridge a bit too long, except this was milky-white and warm. If it was the only alcohol on offer I think I could develop a taste for it.

We had something resembling central heating in our room that night, being the chimney from the kitchen stove below us, running up through one corner. It was becoming cool enough now to be very welcome. Unfortunately, once dinner was finished it went cold.

The toilet was reached by clawing our way back down the now dark passageway by headlamp, across the open dining space and down another passage to two bolt holes containing a squat toilet each and a bucket under a cold water tap. It was also the only place to wash. As I crossed the dining room a small noise alerted me to two bodies asleep on a mud bench by the wall and I realised one of them was Abhinav having to share the limited space with another porter. I entered the toilet room, bolted the door, and as I prepared to wash my face and clean my teeth before bed, my light fell upon the bucket of water in which floated a tiny, dead mouse. It's testimony to how immune to squalor, or exhausted I was, that I used the same water to wash my face. It was probably freshly dead, it was very small, it was a mouse. I simply didn't care, but Neville gasped in disbelief as though I had just flirted with the risk of contracting the plague.

"Why didn't you flush it?" he asked.

"Then I would have had to pick it up."

"I can't believe you washed in the same water as a dead mouse." I shrugged.

When I visited the toilet a few hours later, someone had fished it out and left it lying, stiff and bloodless on the concrete. Why didn't they flush it? I thought. Then someone tried to open the door on me and I banged back on it in frustrated fury.

CHAPTER 25

Chhuksang

Now we were backtracking, and with nothing new to see, the novelty had worn off and I just wanted clean hair, warmth, comfort, different food, and for Neville's clothes to stop smelling like rancid milk.

Soon after we left Shyanmochen, we fell into step with a man and his train of loaded donkeys. I don't know whether Abhinav knew him, but he disappeared with him down the trail for a while, re-emerging on one of the donkeys, a thin mat for a saddle, and a simple piece of rope for reins, thonged feet hanging loosely. The hollow clanging of the donkey's bells joined the music of the clear horse bells.

Thus we rode back into Samar and had tea at the same tea house. Out in the walled yard were the same man and young girl sitting breaking rocks as though they hadn't moved. It was like a video tape in reverse. We travelled down the same narrow track hugging the cliff, past the never-visited village of Ghyakar, and arrived back in the same sunny dining room at the lodge in Tsele in time for lunch.

Gone was the frisson that had sparked off everything as we encountered it for the first time. The land that had bristled with the magic of the new and unknown had now become familiar. Which meant one thing:

I'd accomplished what I'd set out to do. I had discovered Mustang and its "walled city" for myself, I'd seen what Michel Peissel saw and experienced the same journey, albeit without the threat of Khampa warriors. I didn't have to wonder any more. It was real. It wasn't a magical kingdom, a lost and mysterious place. It was a place where people suffered the same worries and aspirations we all share: worries for their prosperity, worries for their children, at the mercy of the gods, the weather and malevolent or otherwise foreign influences. There was no more to discover and I was ready to return to the comforts I was used to, but at the same time, I knew I was leaving behind something I would probably never find again: true silence.

As though he had read my mind, when we arrived in Chhuksang, Pradeep took us down to our room, which was in a newly built section of the lodge and proudly showed us our ensuite: a fully tiled bathroom with pedestal toilet, hot shower and sink, all properly plumbed. He grinned from ear to ear when we showed our delight.

"I book this when we come through here first time. I thought maybe you like this," he said.

I luxuriated in the hot shower and then sat outside on the wall overlooking the kitchen garden and fields in the sun to let my hair dry. In my notes I wrote:

> "We have finally left behind for good all that accommodation that resembles a cowshed."

After showering and some tea and biscuits we set out to see our last Upper Mustang village. A small dog that belonged to the lodge and to whom I gave some rare affection, decided he would accompany us. He followed us along the path and down the to river, which we walked across, easily jumping the shallow rivulets. At this the dog baulked now as though unwilling to get its feet wet, although it went back and forth trying to find another way, eventually giving up.

Chhuksang sits on two sides of the Narshing Khola. We walked up into what seemed a deserted village although there were some signs that people lived there. A lot of the buildings were ruins. Dark passageways ran under and between them but it had an eery feeling and when, as we ventured up one passageway and into a closed courtyard, a dog began growling menacingly from somewhere within, we quickly retreated. We walked back towards the river and followed the path up to a suspension bridge, beside which was growing corn. The cobs were long past the time they would usually be picked for eating. The husks were dry and peeling and the ears were shrivelled. I wondered whether they were grown only for animal feed having never seen corn eaten on our travels.

On the other side of the river was a school, busy with the noise of children. This was something we hadn't seen since Lo Manthang when school children filled the streets after school in the afternoon. We continued uphill to some caves, but entering one, found a padlocked trapdoor at the top of the ladder. We clambered up onto the roof of a ruined building—where a satellite dish had been mounted—then back along the path to our lodge. Below us, Abhinav and another boy with shirts off were soaping themselves under a tap. They looked up as we passed. Abhinav grinned and the other boy called out "Namaste". I noted his packet of cigarettes sitting on the wall with his shirt.

That night, we were joined once again by the Dutch couple from Shyanmochen, and we got to know a bit more about them. Both were social workers, he working with lonely seniors to provide opportunities for socialising, she working in domestic violence. And being one of thirteen children, she had had no desire to have any of her own. They had travelled with the same guide many times and he was now taking them to visit his village and meet his family. In another corner of the dining room were two German girls, their guide and porter, studying the map and anxiously asking which villages ahead had electricity. We quietly snickered at these "rookies" and sipped our rum. They then sat down to a card game called Black Peter. They had a whole box of different games and said we were welcome to borrow any, so Neville and I, and the Dutch couple sat down to a game of Ludo, although the Germans called it by their English translation: "People Don't Get Furious". Pradeep and Dipak had joined the other guides and porters in the kitchen, but Dipak, clutching his raksi, came and sat with us for a while and watched us play.

"Do you have this game in Nepal?" I asked him.

"No," he laughed, and continued watching us intently.

As we played, we chatted about what we'd seen on our travels. The Dutch couple said they thought the King of Lo would never return to his palace in Lo Manthang, being so old now, and that it would be turned into a museum. I hoped not. The palace being turned into a museum would add to the risk of Lo Manthang itself becoming just a remote museum, too difficult a place for the inhabitants to live any more, but with perfectly restored gompas, and the annual Tiji festival just a spectacle to draw tourists whose trekking permit money went straight into the coffers of the government far away in Kathmandu.

CHAPTER 26

The Final Leg

Pradeep had us set out by seven the next morning because we would be walking into the wind as it came up and he wanted to avoid the worst of it. It was our last day of trekking and we were heading back to Jomsom. I gave the small dog a last bit of affection before mounting my horse and riding out of town, but the dog decided he liked the attention and followed. The Dutch couple were heading in our direction and we all kept looking back to this little fellow, something the size of a corgi, as he faithfully pattered along behind us. If it hadn't been such a logistical nightmare I would have seriously considered stealing the dog and taking him back to Australia with me as he seemed starved of affection and obviously liked the idea of leaving home. When Dervla Murphy left Nepal after her stint with Tibetan refugees in the sixties, she took a small dog with her, but in those days you could just put the dog on your lap in the plane, and Ireland's quarantine laws probably weren't as stringent as Australia's. But when we'd been travelling for about half an hour and the dog was still trotting after us, I really started to regret ever touching him. We were slightly ahead of the Dutch couple and I turned back to see they'd taken a short rest by the gates of the organic apple orchard and the dog was now with them. That was the last I saw of him and I hoped he eventually made it back to Chhuksang. A couple of months after we returned home, a snow leopard destroyed a whole flock of goats there, so I don't think it would have been safe for a small dog to go wandering far from home.

By the time we reached Kagbeni the wind had started to pick up, and by Ekla Batti strong gusts were tearing at the trees and rippling the flags on the pole near the ACAP sign. This large sign was purpose built in hinged panels to withstand the wind, and they now creaked violently. A Mustang version of lasagne was proudly served to us in the sunny dining room at the lodge and the fresh tomato slices on top heralded the nearing end of our bland trekking diet.

Before we left home, a friend suggested I download some podcasts to listen to while we travelled, but while I did and I had listened to them sometimes during the night, I wanted to be present in my surroundings, to absorb everything I saw, heard and felt. Now, I felt differently. I'd seen this part of the trip and I was tired of riding a horse. So I plugged in my earphones and turned on a podcast only to find the wind made it impossible to hear anything. It blasted around my ears and pelted dust and sand at my face. If I turned my head sideways I could just hear, but then couldn't see where I was going, so I had to admit defeat and turn it off. And so we travelled for the last two hours, heads down, grim-faced, tired, and a bit sick of each other.

As we rode wearily into Jomsom, Abhinav began to gee up the horses; this was his home town and I can only assume he was either letting everyone know he was back and showing off, or taking the opportunity to try and unseat me one last time. I kept almost losing my balance each time the horse broke into a trot and by the time we pulled up back at the Monalisha Guest House I was so fed up that I immediately dismounted and gave the poor horse a shove in the side. Dipak laughed, Abhinav grinned. I was done with horse-riding for life.

When we'd unloaded everything, Neville handed me the 4000 rupees we'd agreed to give Abhinav and just as he was about to lead the horses away I appeared and handed him the money. He stared at the pile of notes in utter astonishment.

"This is for you, ok?" I said, patting him on the shoulder. All he could do was look at the money, open-mouthed. "See you next time."

He broke into to a broad grin and looked at Pradeep and Dipak.

"And don't spend it on cigarettes," I added, and still grinning ear to ear, this bombastic seventeen-year-old boy stuffed the notes into the pocket of his torn, filthy jeans, turned the horses about, led them down a side street and disappeared. I felt a little sad that I would probably never see him again.

That night, a freshly-washed Pradeep and Dipak joined us for one last dinner in the dining room. We drank a lot of beer and rum that night, and tucked into meat and fresh vegetables. Dipak happily shovelled in a mound of rice and dahl, gladly accepting more as it was heaped onto his plate by the generous host.

After we'd finished eating and were watching a documentary about Mt. Kailash on the TV (with Pradeep adding some commentary), two young girls entered the dining room looking for dinner. They were from Australia and New Zealand and we asked them if they were going or coming from trekking. No, they said, they'd just caught the bus up from Pokhara to see what was here. As they pored over the quite extensive menu, the host, who probably thought he'd done with cooking by that time of the night, made suggestions. In an attempt to hurry the decision-making, he described his specialty dish, a Nepalese lasagne, full of fresh tomato and cheese.

"Mmm, that sounds good," drawled the Australian, "but I'm not really doing lactose at the moment."

"Well I'm off to bed," I said, and stood up from the table. The adventure was over.

CHAPTER 27

Pokhara Again

There was always the risk of being stranded in Jomsom due to inclement weather, so we were up by five the next morning in the hope of getting a flight. Though our trek was at an end, Dipak still attended us diligently, serving us hot milk tea in the gloom of the interior courtyard downstairs and then insisting on carrying both large packs by himself to the airport. As we walked the short distance we passed women selling bags of dried apples laid out on rugs along the street. The sky was overcast and we knew if it didn't clear we might be staying another night.

The waiting area at the airport was a lively scene with large family groups of Indians. They fly to Jomsom on their way to pilgrimage at Muktinath, an hour and a half jeep ride away. Here they bathe in 108 sacred fountains, despite the freezing water, and see the flame of natural gas that burns above another spring. The shrine is sacred to both Hindus and Buddhists and was another place Padmasambhava meditated on his way to Tibet. Saligrams were for sale at the small canteen and the Indians clustered eagerly at the window. Having bought them, they undid their newspaper wrapping and stood admiring and comparing. Mine was safely tucked away in the depths of my bag and I felt a bit smug that mine was bigger and better than the ones at the airport, but also a little guilty; if these people regarded them with such reverence, maybe I should too.

When the all-clear for flying comes through at Jomsom and down in Pokhara, the whole airport springs to life, because there may only be a short window and they want to get as many flights there and back as possible. So suddenly we were being ushered into separate male-female curtained booths to be frisked. I was clutching my helmet because I just couldn't be bothered packing it, but as soon as the guard saw it she shook her head.

"You can't take this on the plane," she said.

I hated that helmet.

I poked my head out the back of the booth and called to Pradeep.

"She says I can't carry it on," I told him.

Without a word, he took the cursed helmet and carried it over to the checked baggage where he clipped it onto his own bag. I was going to miss having Pradeep around to solve our problems.

Twenty minutes later we stepped out into the warm humidity of the Pokhara valley.

CHAPTER 28

Escaping Kathmandu

In Upper Mustang we'd heard fragments of news that all was not well in the rest of Nepal. In the two weeks since that night in Tsele, when everyone had clustered eagerly around the television watching the first constitution being ratified in the parliament, all hell had broken loose on the border with India. The Madhesi, an ethnic group who live in the border region, felt they were unrepresented within the constitution and began protesting. Since they are ethnically more closely related to the Indians over the border than to the other ethnic groups in Nepal, India were sympathetic to their cause. Forty people were killed in clashes with police, and a blockade was formed on the bridge that crosses the border. The Nepalese government blamed India for the blockade, but India claimed it was Nepal's fault as the protesters made it too dangerous for them to cross. Since Nepal is landlocked, it relies on India for nearly all of its supplies, especially petrol for vehicles and gas for cooking.

We returned to Kathmandu to find it slowly grinding to a halt. Queues for fuel stretched for blocks and was being rationed, and restaurants were having to curtail their menus because they were running out of gas. Hospitals were running out of medical supplies and, according to one report, the Bir Hospital had resorted to cooking for its 300 patients over a wood fire outside. The rush to buy electric cookers began overloading the already inadequate electricity supply, causing more blackouts. But for the first time in our experience, the streets were quieter and the air clearer; the Himalayas, usually hidden by thick smog, stood out clearly above the hills enclosing the valley.

Taxis were becoming scarce as the fuel supply dried up, but there were a couple of things I needed to do before we left Nepal.

We had to walk out to the main road before we found a taxi. After some negotiation, we agreed to pay six times the usual fare, if the driver would take us across the river to Patan, wait for us and bring us back. I was going to visit Jay and his mother, Sunita.

The director of the centre led us into the the room where the most severely disabled children were cared for and there, as though no time had passed, lay Jay. He wore the same yellow jumper I'd left him in, a hand-me-down from one of my sons, now torn but roughly restitched. When Sunita entered the room and saw me, a smile spread across her face and she held her hands up in a silent "Namaste". She sat down on the floor and sat Jay up, cradling his skeletal body against her tiny frame. His unsmiling face lolled sideways and a thick, wet, feeble cough made him jerk. I handed her a new bag of hand-me-down clothing and she quietly put it behind her. It's not customary for Nepalese to make great shows of gratitude, believing the true benefit lies with the giver. As we sat drinking glasses of sweet black tea Sunita reached under the fraying collar of Jay's jumper and drew out a black string on which was tied the medal I had fastened around her neck at the hospital.

I had expected Jay to die three years before when I left him in Patan hospital but here he was, albeit still struggling for breath through lungs full of fluid, his devoted mother still massaging his contracted, bony hands, and lovingly smoothing the sides of his face with her small hands.

Twelve months later a post came up on Facebook with a photo of Jay. He was held up by Sunita, her face next to his, one arm across his left shoulder, the other hand clutching his right wrist. His face was grey and his lips drained of colour. His dull eyes underlined by shadows looked to the side of the picture. The caption read: Jay you are no more with us. Rest in Peace.

The other visit I needed to make was to Sabina with whom I'd worked at the disabled centre, who had entreated me to come to the hospital to support Jay and Sunita and who, along with her mother, had had to move out of her home because it was damaged by the earthquake. She wanted to show me the damage in the hope that we could help in some way.

Sabina was waiting for us near our old favourite cafe. An attractive woman of forty, she was immaculately dressed in traditional loose pyjama pants with a salwar kameez over the top and a long scarf, her long hair falling like black silk down her back. She led us through the bustling, dusty, narrow streets of Patan through a low doorway and into a small courtyard.

The only house I'd been into in Kathmandu was our host family's and while I knew they were relatively wealthy compared to most Nepalese, until then I hadn't realised how much wealthier. Their two-storey home, though an uninspiring grey box of concrete-rendered brick, (with steel girders sticking out the top for the next storey to be added if necessary) was light and airy, with glazed windows. It also had two bathrooms, both with pedestal toilets, a kitchen with a fridge and sink, and an automatic washing machine; all possible because it had the one thing most homes don't: running water. Poorer people must collect water from the common stone taps for cooking and washing; some have one tap on the outside of their house.

Sabina led us across the courtyard, through a low doorway into almost total darkness, and up a narrow, wooden stairway.

"This is the apartment we are renting since the earthquake," she told us.

We emerged into a room about the size of an average Australian bedroom. It had two unglazed windows that looked out on the courtyard below, one single bed against the far wall and a mattress on the floor at right angles to the bed. On the wall opposite the windows was a flat-screen television plugged into a power-board along with two mobile phones. On the ledge above was an assorted collection of objects: a framed black and white photo of Sabina's mother as a child with her parents; a small calendar; a colour photo of women dressed in red saris; a small torch; a plant growing in a jar of water; and a small, red, portable speaker. The dirt floor was covered in mismatched offcuts of carpet, and sheets of plastic. The wires from the one powerpoint snaked up the wall, across the ceiling and out through the window. A light-switch for the one fluorescent bulb hung loose from the ceiling. In a narrow alcove was a pedal sewing machine on which sat a small stack of cut material.

"My mother makes baby clothes to sell in the market, but is not much money," Sabina told me.

Her mother smiled at us but could speak no English. She picked up the small speaker and switched it on. It played an Indian song sung by a male voice.

"Sai Baba," Sabina explained, (the famous Indian guru). "My mother likes him very much."

The tinny music continued. Sabina's mother indicated we should sit down so, there being no chairs, I sat on the bed and Neville on the mattress.

"Would you like tea?" Sabina asked.

Feeling it would be rude to say no, we both said yes, and then regretted it. Sabina and her mother looked at each other and quickly disappeared. Steps were heard on the stairs and noises could be heard from the pitch dark space on the other side of the wall. After about ten minutes they emerged bearing two cups of milky, sweet tea, and two saucers with a fried egg on each. While they sat on the floor smiling at us, we drank our tea and ate our eggs with as much gratitude as we could muster, knowing they had had to go out to buy milk for the tea and use precious gas to cook the eggs.

"Now I show you our house."

Sabina led us into the next courtyard and again into almost complete darkness. We climbed another narrow staircase up to a dimly-lit room with a dirt floor and up another until we emerged into an identical dimly-lit space. On the right was the kitchen: a blackened, dirt-covered brick bench with small alcoves for storage and space for a gas-cooker. On the left was an empty room, lighter than all the others because the entire back wall had fallen out. The earthquake aside, it was easy to see why: rotting, splintered beams and crumbling clay bricks clung precariously to the remaining walls and roof. I knew we were standing on equally rotting wood and prayed there would be no tremors.

"This is my mother's room," Sabina told us. "When we were growing up, my four sisters and I slept on the floor below."

I had known Sabina for five years and knew her father was killed in an accident when she was twelve, leaving her mother to raise five girls alone, but I'd never been to her house or thought about the reality of her childhood. Now I could not comprehend how she had grown up in this dark, dank, crumbling building, that it was still her's and her mother's home and that they were desperate to move back into it. When I tried to describe it to people at home, the closest I could come was the space under my house on bare dirt with cobwebby floorboards overhead, but even that was airier and lighter.

We climbed down the dark narrow stairs and out into the bright sunshine.

"Would you like to come upstairs again?" Sabina asked.

I looked up at the dark windows of their flat.

"Our taxi is waiting."

She nodded.

Ducking out through the doorway of the courtyard, we walked away through the narrow streets, climbed into the taxi, and headed back to our hotel.

With taxis fast disappearing off the streets, and the hotel no longer able to run its shuttle service, getting to the airport was going to be a problem. We caught Ganesh, the tourist liaison, in the hotel lobby. He look unusually harassed. We'd heard him the day before explaining to a guest in exasperated tones that no, they couldn't organise a taxi for her the following morning. When we approached him he immediately looked defensive but, recognising us as repeat customers, quickly ushered us into his office and closed the door.

"Let me make a phone call," he said after indicating for us to sit down.

After a quick conversation in Nepali, he put the phone down.

"My friend can take you for 4000 rupees."

"Ok," Neville replied.

"Don't blame me sir," he said, "There's nothing I can do…"

"Ganesh, it's ok," Neville reassured him.

That evening a very new four-wheel-drive pulled up outside the lobby.

"Where did you get the fuel?" asked Neville.

"Black market," said Ganesh's friend.

Back home I hung the horse bell by my front door. I occasionally ring it to remind me of that clear sound that accompanied us on our journey through Mustang. The black saligram sits on the hall table along with three stones—red, white, and grey like the stripes on the chortens—I picked up below the red cliffs in Tragmar. I sometimes pull out the striped apron and feel its tightly woven colourful stripes and think of the women sweeping the streets of Lo Manthang, herding cows, cooking over wood and gas fires. And when I pulled the gold and silver painted mandala I bought in Lo Manthang from our artist-guide, Tashi, out of its piece of PVC piping, out came the smell of manure.

I have these things to prove, if only to myself, that I once rode a nameless horse to an ancient, remote, city on the Tibetan plateau. My journey stands in pale contrast to the heroic journeys of Dervla Murphy and Freya Stark, but I still overcame fear and self-doubt. I achieved the destination I had given myself on leaving my home town forever, and while the pain will never fully leave, I know I could never return to Bellingen to live. There are few people there that I know and the town and

I have changed too much. I think about the exiled Tibetans, longing for a home that no longer exists as they knew it, and that may be unrecognisable soon, and the Tibetans who wish they could leave. I think about the people from Lo Manthang, those Tibetans who have not had their culture ravaged by an invading force, but who have nevertheless left their home in search of all those things the outside world offers: education, travel, money. I imagine at times they too long for their home, high up on the windswept plateau, its quiet, its smells, the music, the food, but know, like me, if they do return, it will not be to the same place.

Home is like a sand mandala; built over years with layer upon layer of memories, only to be one day swept away.

AUTHOR'S NOTES

The names of the villages of Upper Mustang have been rendered into English from their original languages and therefore there are various versions, none of which is strictly correct. Lo Manthang should more accurately be called Lo Monthang but is more usually spelled the former way. Similarly, Tragmar is also written as Drakmar or Dhakmar, Shyenmochen as Syanbochen, Tsele as Chele and so on.

Our guides and the people from the children's disability centre were unaware that our conversations might be published. I have therefore changed their names.

BIBLIOGRAPHY

Aryal, A., Brunton, D., Pandit, R., Kumar Rai, R., Shrestha, U. B., Lama, N., & Raubenheimer, D. (2013). Rangelands, Conflicts, and Society in the Upper Mustang Region, Nepal. *Mountain Research and Development*, 33(1), 11-18. doi:10.1659/mrd-journal-d-12-00055.1

Craig, S. (2004). A Tale of Two Temples: Culture, Capital, and Community in Mustang, Nepal. *European Bulletin of Himalayan Research*, (27), 11-36.

Craig, S. (2016). *Horses Like Lightning: A Story of Passage Through the Himalayas*. Boston, MA: Wisdom Publications.

David-Néel, A., Rowan, D., & Dalai Lama. (1927). *My Journey to Lhasa*. New York: Harper Perennial.

Devkota, F. (2013). Climate Change and its socio-cultural impact in the Himalayan region of Nepal – A Visual Documentation. *Anthrovision*, (1.2). doi:10.4000/anthrovision.589

Hagen, T., & Charleston, B. M. (1973). *Nepal*. London: Hale.

Holland, P. (2012). *Riding the Trains in Japan: Travels in the Sacred and Supermodern East*. Melbourne: Transit Lounge

Hopkirk, P. (2006). *Trespassers on the Roof of the World: The Race for Lhasa*. London: John Murray.

Jackson, D. P. (2002). *The Mollas of Mustang*. New Delhi: Paljor Publications.

Kirkpatrick, W. (1811). *An Account of the Kingdom of Nepaul [sic] in the year 1793*. London: William Miller.

Knaus, J. K. (2000). *Orphans of the Cold War: America and the Tibetan Struggle for Survival*. New York: PublicAffairs.

Lustgarten, A. (2008) *China's Great Train: Beijing's Drive West and the Campaign to Remake Tibet*. New York: Times Books/Henry Holt

Matthiesen, P., & Laird, T. (1996). *East of Lo Monthang: In the land of Mustang*. Boston: Shambhala.

Mayhew, B., Bindloss, J., & Staff. (2009). *Lonely Planet: Trekking in the Nepal Himalaya*. Australia: Lonely Planet Publications.

Murphy, D. (1966). *Tibetan Foothold*. London: John Murray

Murphy, D. (1967). *The Waiting Land: A Spell in Nepal*. London: John Murray

Peissel, M. (1968). *Mustang: a Lost Tibetan Kingdom*. London: Collins.

Rijnhart, Susie Carson (1901). *With Tibetans in Tent and Temple*. Chicago: Fleming H. Revell

Shrestha, D., & Whitaker, M. (2012). *Mustang - Paradise Found*. Kathmandu: Himalayan Maphouse.

Snellgrove, D. L. (2012). *Himalayan Pilgrimage: A study of Tibetan religion by a traveller through Western Nepal*. Bangkok, Thailand: Orchid Press.

Snook, B. et al (2018). *Brothers and Sisters: Coping With Grief and Loss*. Brisbane: Glass House Books

Sun, S. (2008). *A Year in Tibet*. London: Harper Press.

Thapa, M. (1992). *Mustang Bhot in Fragments*. Lalitpur: Himal Books.

Tucci, G., & Fussell, D. (2003). *Journey to Mustang 1952*. Kathmandu: Ratna Pustak Bhandar.

Xinran, Tyldesley, E., & Lovell, J. (2004) *Sky Burial*. London: Chatto & Windus

ACKNOWLEDGMENTS

This book began as the major project for my masters degree and was first developed with my supervisor, the acclaimed Australian author Patrick Holland, who gave me to believe it might actually be worth publishing. Thanks also to Australian writer Anna Krien, one of my university tutors, who told me I could write.

The fledgling manuscript was accepted into the 2017 Hardcopy Manuscript Development Programme run by the Australian Writers' Centre in Canberra where editor Nadine Davidoff refused to let me get away with just calling a travel narrative and forced me to explore why I went on the journey. After two edits Nadine helped me turn it into the book it is today.

Special thanks to American anthropologist Sienna Craig, an expert on Upper Mustang, especially its horses and traditional medicine, for answering my many questions.

Thanks to Zoe Krupka (who contributed the second chapter, "Holding Hands in the Dark: Unburdening a Grieving Child" to the anthology *Brothers and Sisters)*, Patrick Holland, Manjushree Thapa, and Sienna Craig for allowing me to quote from their work; their books are listed in the bibliography and are highly recommended reading.

Thanks also to my friends, in particular Michele Harris and Dr. Paula Loveday, for being my beta readers and providing feedback and encouragement, and Kirsten for coming on my second trip to Nepal.

Last but not least, thanks goes to my husband, Neville, without whom I would never have made it anywhere, but especially to Lo Manthang and back, and to my three sons, Christopher, Daniel and Thomas for enduring that first trip to Nepal in 2010, which started the whole thing. Special thanks to Thomas for not trashing the joint while we were gone.

www.ingramcontent.com/pod-product-compliance
Lightning Source LLC
Chambersburg PA
CBHW020410080526
44584CB00014B/1264